Joshua

SO-CNF-303

GOD'S FORMULA
for Passionate Living

Pure Joy

by Matt Tullos, Paul Turner,
and Kristi Cherry

*Though you have not seen him, you love him; and even
though you do not see him now, you believe in him and
are filled with an inexpressible and glorious joy.*
−1 Peter 1:8

LifeWay Press
Nashville, Tennessee

This book is a resource in the "Personal Life"
category of the Christian Growth Study Plan.
Course CG-0790
Dewey Decimal Classification: 241.66
Subject Heading: SEXUAL ETHICS / LIFESTYLES / YOUTH

Unless otherwise indicated, Scripture quotations are from
the Holy Bible, New International Version. Copyright © 1973, 1978,
1984 by International Bible Society. Used by permission.

Printed in the United States of America.

Student Ministry Publishing
LifeWay Church Resources
One LifeWay Plaza
Nashville, TN 37234-0174

To order additional copies of this resource:
WRITE LifeWay Church Resources Customer Service,
One LifeWay Plaza, Nashville, TN 37234-0113;
FAX (615) 251- 5933; PHONE 1-800-458-2772;
EMAIL to CustomerService@lifeway.com;
ONLINE at www.lifeway.com;
or visit the LifeWay Christian Store serving you.

We believe that the Bible has God for its author; salvation for its end;
and truth, without any mixture of error, for its matter and that all
Scripture is totally true and trustworthy. The 2000 statement of The
Baptist Faith and Message is our doctrinal guideline.

CONTENTS

FOREWORD

I confess. Sometimes it can be tough to live the Christian life, and doing it on my own is absolutely impossible. Pure joy is one of those things that can be accomplished if we realize that it is not meant to be done all by ourselves. Too many students, and adults for that matter, have decided that God never intended for them to be able to achieve this life of pure joy. The big problem with that kind of thinking is that the Bible is full of examples of folks who really did experience pure joy in their lives!

So here is what to expect from this little book. Are you ready for this?

1. It is "in your face" kind of stuff. You can complete this study and come out on the other end unfazed, but that will be hard to do. While working through this book, you will be challenged to think, learn, and grow.

2. No one is expecting you to live an obedient life on your own. This book will give you a comprehensive look at purity and ways to become accountable to others in pursuing this life of pure joy.

3. The authors are praying that you grasp the concepts of living your life in obedience to Christ. *Pure Joy* will present these concepts, but it will be your choice to put them into action in your life.

4. Even though this book is marked with the True Love Waits logo, it deals with living a life that is pure beyond sexual purity. It addresses purity in relationships, passions, thoughts, habits, and other areas.

5. This book is designed to move you towards obedience and experiencing pure joy in your life. It is not intended to hammer you over the head and make you think you can never have the pure joy God wants to give to you.

Our hope is that you will encounter Christ as you never have before and learn the joy of living the life of purity that God created you to live.

—Paul Turner, co-chairperson of True Love Waits

INTRODUCTION

There are a lot of reasons Satan wants to keep you away from this book:
- He wants to steal your peace.
- He wants to chain you to a defeated lifestyle.
- He wants to escort you to an early grave.
- He wants to distract you from your mission.
- He wants to corrupt the blessing of a holy life.
- He's determined to fill your life with self-doubt and shame.
- He wants to curse your future children.
- He wants to cloud your vision.
- He wants to convince you that you don't deserve God's plan.
- He wants you strapped with addiction.
- He wants to immobilize you.
- He wants to offer you cheap thrills in exchange for your eternal passion.
- He wants to keep you hopeless, helpless, and violated.
- He wants to make you a stumbling block.
- He wants to embarrass you.
- He knows that people who live a passionate, Christian life are a direct threat to his mission.
- He trembles to think of a generation of pure prayer warriors storming the gates of his kingdom.

There is one reason why Jesus wants you to experience the truth of this study: He wants you to have an overflowing, victorious, everlasting life!

We challenge you. We *dare* you to discover and live out the principles contained in this little book. One thing is certain, you'll never regret it.

As a part of your daily quiet time, work though *Pure Joy* one chapter per week. It won't take long for you to complete it. Studying the material will heighten the opportunities for you to experience incredible breakthroughs!

Along with this book and your Bible, we recommend that you use a journal as a tool in the *Pure Joy* experience. A journal gives you unlimited space to record the discoveries and commitments you are making. Keeping a personal journal is a way for you to record God's work in your life. It will be something you'll cherish as the years go by. You'll also be able to trace the undeniable presence of God in your life. Keep your journal honest, private, and frequently utilized.

A Prayer of Beginning

Lord, You have given me this moment. Tomorrow is not promised, and yesterday will never come again. You have placed me here at this point in my life to receive the principles contained in this book. I believe that You have a plan for me. I now ask You, Lord, to reveal to me the secret to passionate, holy living. I know that I can't experience it outside of my relationship with You. I'm asking for You to take authority right now. Give me the courage to see and acknowledge where I am and where You want me to be. Thank You for this invitation to experience pure joy and passionate living. You are all I need. In the name of Jesus, Amen.

Purity
Self-Portrait

Kerstin couldn't harness her emotions as she sat on the couch next to her friends in her home Bible study group and spoke with unforgettable honesty of a relationship that ended two years ago, before she moved to Amarillo.

"The relationship was going great, and neither one of us planned to do the things we did. We didn't plan on getting in too deep, but we thought we were in love. I remember that our parents weren't too cool on us spending a lot of time together, and that seemed to draw us even closer. It's crazy how the mind works when you think you've met the one you want to spend the rest of your life with. After about three months, we finally gave in. But I can tell you from experience that it didn't draw us any closer. After a while our relationship was totally … well … deflated. We were like strangers to each other. It even destroyed our friendship."

Kerstin wiped a tear that rolled down her face.

"Well, I still *do* miss the friendship. It was taken from me. It was like having sex destroyed everything that we had; and believe me, we had a whole lot going for us before then. I know that Christ has forgiven me, but I'm having a hard time forgiving myself. I wasted a precious part of myself on someone that I'll probably never see again in my life. And every time that I'm around a guy, I feel guilty—almost like I'm not clean. It's like when I go to church, Satan shoves the mistake right in front of my face."

Silence pervaded the room. The students gathered around her and prayed. I watched in amazement at the honesty of her struggle.

YOUR INVITATION TO PURE JOY
In truth, Kerstin's struggle is typical of the remorse that many teens experience as they get a closer view of the holiness of God. It provokes a flood of questions:

- How can someone in this culture remain pure?
- What is purity?
- Is there really joy without sex?
- Can I be delivered from the haunting memories of past failures?
- Am I still loved as deeply by God after I fail?
- How can I break the addictive cycle of impurity?
- How can I overcome the devil and his seductive traps and strategies?
- How does worship dissolve strongholds and oppressive thoughts?
- How can I understand the source of my desires?
- Why is making a public commitment to purity so important?

This study was created to help you reach the understanding that purity is an attainable goal in the life of a follower of Christ. We can offer Jesus our very best if we are consumed by His passion and powered by His Spirit. Purity is not for the unemotional, weak, or ambiguously religious student. It is an outgrowth of a single-minded, focused, passionate follower of Christ who has a daily drive to know God fully. But if you aren't there yet, don't be discouraged. Instead, ask God to use this study as the springboard for your journey to purity.

Read *Luke 10:40-41*.
What does this story teach us about our focus? _____

_____

_____

_____

_____

_____

Are you more like Martha, running around trying to do a lot of things; or are you more like her sister Mary, sitting at Jesus' feet, listening to what He has to say? _____

Dave has it all together, right? He is a junior in high school, where he is very involved in the Fellowship of Christian Athletes, the French Club, and the Debate Team. Dave is also a committed Christian who feels called to minister in a lot of unique situations. He has a car payment, a part-time job, and a golden retriever. And with all of these plates seemingly spinning simultaneously, he manages to have a relationship with

Jana. Dave's life is exhausting, exhilarating, and stressful—but never boring. Even though he is successful and popular, he often feels dreadfully alone.

The busyness of his life seems to be a monster of his own creation. Sometimes at night when he's trying to sleep, he begins to wonder why he feels so incomplete and alone. On the outside, he looks like a model success story, worthy of a feature article in a Christian youth magazine. But as he contemplates his life and his direction, something seems out of place. His symptoms appear not on the public main stage of life, but in the private closets. Usually when he finds free time, he is driven toward the Internet. Despite his commitment toward the Christian life and his desire to serve, he quickly finds himself muddled in a web of pornography.

His relationship with Jana is also a cause for concern. Both of them have a compelling desire to be a part of God's work in their community and church. However, Dave has a sexual desire that seems to be out of control. The more time they are together, the more difficult it is to not give in to temptation. The more intimate Jana and Dave become, the more they are gripped with a sense of shame and failure. Dave is a committed believer, and yet he is a victim to a growing compulsion that seems to be overpowering him.

Read _2 Samuel 11:1–5_. How does Dave's story relate to King David's struggle? _____

_____

_____

King David experienced restlessness and emptiness similar to Dave's. This lack of peace ultimately drove him to commit unspeakable sins that put up a wall between him and God. The concept of purity is more than just a sexual barometer. Purity is a vital part of every aspect of your life, but it is not something that you can attain on your own. Many people have attempted to be pure out of their own power, only to fail. The power to be pure can be received only through a passionate relationship with Jesus Christ, allowing Him complete and total access to every public and private area of your life.

But he said to me, "My grace is sufficient for you, for my power is made perfect in weakness." Therefore I will boast all the more gladly about my weaknesses, so that Christ's power may rest on me (2 Cor. 12:9).

In a culture where we live like we're racing in the Indy 500, few people slow down and spend a substantial amount of time examining their life. Self-examination is the first step to achieving pure joy—it is not an option. Making a change in your spiritual life is impossible without understanding who you are, where you have been, and why you do the things you do. This is the first pivotal step away from a defeated, habit-driven life. We challenge you to take whatever time is necessary to evaluate where you are so that God can begin His work in your life.

SPECIAL

GOD LOVES US THE WAY WE ARE BUT HE LOVES US TOO MUCH TO LEAVE US THAT WAY. —LEIGHTON FORD

WHERE AM I?

1. **We all have heard the phrase "time is money." If your week was compared to money, and every week of your life was equal to $500, how much of that $500 would be spent in spiritual renewal per week?** _____
2. **What amount would be spent on TV and music?** _____
3. **What amount of time, if figured in dollars, would be spent in exhausting, nonproductive activities?** _____

Colossians 3:17 says, And whatever you do, whether in word or deed, do it all in the name of the Lord Jesus, giving thanks to God the Father through him.

I find it difficult to give God complete access to these things in my life: _____
_____
_____
_____

WHERE HAVE I BEEN?

Perhaps the most difficult thing for Christians to do is to forgive themselves for their sinful acts and wrong choices of the past. Using your journal or a separate sheet of paper, spend time contemplating and answering the following questions.

What events or things in your past have made you hesitant to even try to be pure before God? _____

_____

_____

_____

Keep in mind that there may be events that you had no control over. Perhaps you were abused as a child or your parents divorced a few years ago, and the hurt that you feel seems overwhelming and impossible to escape. Even in the most ideal circumstances, people carry a sense of burden that they receive from unanticipated grief, sorrow, and crisis.

Are there any areas or issues of unforgiveness in your life that have driven a wedge between you and God? _____

_____

What idols are present in your life? _____

_____

_____

_____

Idols are things that you consider to be more important than or equally important as your relationship with God. Common idols include food, a quest to look perfect, drugs, alcohol, pornography, money, escapism, relationships, or addiction to entertainment. Some of these things, such as money and personal appearance, are situationally evil, not inherently evil. Money itself is not evil. In fact, it can be a great tool in ministry. *The love of money is a root of all kinds of evil (1 Tim. 6:10).* That lust for money has the ability to bring calamity and destruction in your life. It's not wrong to want to appear attractive, but if you devote an overwhelming amount of time and effort to looking perfect, you might be placing more faith in your looks than you do in God.

If you spent the time to evaluate yourself using these questions, it is likely that the Lord may have brought you into a new understanding of your spiritual condition. The good news is that God has the ability to completely bring you into purity!

Read and meditate upon the following Scriptures.

If we confess our sins, he is faithful and just and will forgive us our sins and purify us from all unrighteousness (1 John 1:9).

"Come now, let us reason together," says the Lord, "though your sins are like scarlet, they shall be as white as snow; though they are red as crimson, they shall be like wool" (Isa. 1:18).

LOOK!

I COULDN'T LIVE IN PEACE IF I PUT THE SHADOW OF A WILLFUL SIN BETWEEN MYSELF AND GOD.
—GEORGE ELIOT

Bear with each other and forgive whatever grievances you may have against one another. Forgive as the Lord forgave you (Col. 3:13).

As far as the east is from the west, so far has he removed our transgressions from us (Ps. 103:12).

After taking inventory of these questions and your answers, spend time with the Lord confessing those things which are unconfessed in your life. Allow God's truth to sink into your mind. Pray this prayer:

Lord, I praise You for being a God who forgives. I desperately need to know and to understand the depth of Your forgiveness. I confess these areas of my life where I have failed to seek Your forgiveness and to release forgiveness to others. Lord Jesus, more than anything, I want to have a pure and holy life. Cleanse me and make me the holy servant You desire. I understand that I cannot be holy in my own strength. I know that the power to be pure comes only from You. Lord, I am reaching out to You in the best way I know how. I want You to take me, to break me, and to make me over so that I can be a worthy vessel, not for my own glory or self-righteousness, but for Your glory and for Your honor. Thank You for forgiving me. Thank You for your cleansing power. Thank You for the price that You paid so that I can be holy and pure. Give me the strength to live this life in You. In Jesus' name, Amen.

IS THERE A DIFFERENCE BETWEEN HAPPINESS AND JOY?

We hear our friends say things like, "I'm just not happy with my life." We hear a disillusioned husband say, "My wife does not make me happy." There is no doubt that you could make a mile-high stack of books that promise the secret to happiness. So what's the difference between temporal happiness and eternal joy? There is a wide gulf between joy and happiness. The root of the word *happy* is the same root that is used for *happens*. Happiness happens. Many times it's out of our control. A good grade, a sports victory, a flattering remark … all of these things have the ability to make us happy; but happiness alone will never equal joy.

Joy is an eternal satisfaction regardless of circumstance. Joy survives regardless of tragedy, defeat, or isolation. Joy is a God thing. The spark of joy will never be kindled by fortune, fame, a full stomach, or sexual gratification. In a dank, putrid, Roman jail, we find the apostle Paul penning the words, *Rejoice in the Lord always. I will say it again: Rejoice! (Phil. 4:4)* He challenged us to rejoice. Despite our circumstance, despite the pain, despite the situation, we can rejoice. Joy in the life of a Christian is unshakable. It cannot be stopped because it's not a man thing; it is a God thing.

Read *Habakkuk 3:17-18*.
In your own life, what would compare to the disastrous circumstances listed in these verses? _____

_____

_____

_____

When these things happen, will you still be able to rejoice in the Lord? Spend time in prayer this week asking for this God-given joy that is not dependent upon circumstance.

Though you have not seen him, you love him; and even though you do not see him now, you believe in him and are filled with an inexpressible and glorious joy (1 Pet. 1:8).

SATAN'S THREE-PRONGED STRATEGY TO STEAL YOUR JOY

If you are a Christian, you can count on the fact that Satan has proposed a plan for your destruction. He would count it a great accomplishment if he could get you to believe that the Christian life cannot be lived, that it is an impossible task totally devoid of joy.

The Shame Strategy–Read *Revelation 12:10*. Satan's primary mode of operation is accusation. He seeks to destroy your confidence, effectiveness, and faith in God by whispering words of condemnation into your heart. This is the true basis of shame. He will continue to hurl accusations and judgment upon you until *he* is ultimately hurled into the pit!

Yes! ALL HEAVEN IS INTERESTED IN THE CROSS OF CHRIST, ALL HELL TERRIBLY AFRAID OF IT.
—OSWALD CHAMBERS

Here is a list of accusations that Satan would love to slap on you. As you read them, make special note of the ones that have entered your life and sabotaged your effectiveness as a child of God.

You don't have the strength to be pure.
Do you think that God could love you? Of course not.
You are far from perfect.
You are a sinner, and you will continue to sin.
There is nothing you can do about it.
Your parents divorced because of you.
You were a mistake.
How could anyone love you?
Your mind is corrupt, and there is no way you can be transformed.
How do you expect to be accepted by your peers if you don't give in to your natural desires?
You are simply no fun.
You need to stop trying to live a holy life. It's impossible to do that.

Satan's shame strategy is to make you feel like there is something wrong with you as a created being. When God sees things in your life that are ungodly, He lovingly points to them and invites you to repent of those sins and follow Him. The Holy Spirit's work of repentance in your life always works redemptively. In other words, He always provides you an opportunity to begin again. In opposition, Satan's greatest ambition is for you to look at all your sins, worldly thoughts, and wrong choices as being a part of who you are.

Your worst days are never so bad that you are beyond the reach of God's grace. And your best days are never so good that you are beyond the need of God's grace. —Jerry Bridges

Be self-controlled and alert. Your enemy the devil prowls around like a roaring lion looking for someone to devour (1 Pet. 5:8).

Pause now and ask God to begin to remove the shame that Satan has tried to inflict upon you.

God's Promises to Overcome Satan's Shame Strategy:
Those who look to him are radiant; their faces are never covered with shame (Ps. 34:5).

Therefore, brothers, since we have confidence to enter the Most Holy Place by the blood of Jesus,...let us draw near to God with a sincere heart in full assurance of faith, having our hearts sprinkled to cleanse us from a guilty conscience (Heb. 10:19,22).

The Addiction Strategy–Satan's greatest desire for your life is to enslave you in a recurring, regular pattern of sin. He knows that if you carry a burden of shame and helplessness, there is a great chance that this feeling will inhibit you from being all that God called you to be. The shame strategy and the addiction strategy work hand-in-hand. If you are carrying shame, chances are you will fall into an addictive lifestyle. Addiction is chemical, mental, and spiritual. It is the act of habitually turning to anything outside of God for a feeling of satisfaction.

Addiction can start out harmless, affecting just a small portion of your life, and then gradually begin to spread into every aspect of your life. Addiction begins when a person feels empty inside. It's a restlessness that approaches us when we are in the middle of spiritual yearning or turmoil. At that time we have two choices. We can run to God for support and fulfillment, or we can fill our lives with counterfeit fulfillment such as sex, drugs, adrenaline, television, the Internet, or food, just to name a few.

Think now about the things that you have turned to instead of God when you reached a time of emptiness.

When we experience emptiness and give in to sin, it seems gratifying and fulfilling at the time. But shortly after the experience of sin, we begin to feel an overwhelming sense of guilt and shame. Satan tempts us to fulfill our own needs his way, and then he becomes the accuser. He accuses us of committing the very sins that he lured us to commit. Keep in mind that throughout this cycle, God is standing near to us, pleading with us to repent and return to Him. When we run away from Him, we realize how helpless we are and that no act of sacrifice or service can repay the wrongness we feel. The guilt and shame eventually transform into anger. We become angry because we know that we are powerless to overcome our sins. And after this sense of anger, Satan leads us into another period of the addictive cycle. We realize that we have been here before. In fact, this was the place that brought us to commit the sinful act. We realize that we are in a state of even deeper emptiness and loneliness. It is at this point that we are once again tempted to commit sin, and the cycle begins again.

In your personal journal, write about times when you have found yourself in an addictive pattern of sin. Do you see the cycle still at work in your life?

In your journal, write a prayer to the Lord asking Him to protect you from the addiction strategy of Satan.

If you are in this cycle right now, spend some time asking the Lord to deliver you from Satan's stronghold in your life. You will never experience joy and fulfillment within your journey as a Christian unless you are able to cast down these addictive cycles that Satan uses to keep you from total reliance on God.

Abide in Jesus, the sinless one—which means, give up all of self and its life, and dwell in God's will and rest in His strength. This is what brings the power that does not commit sin. —Andrew Murray

God's Promises to Overcome Satan's Addiction Strategy:
*Flee from sexual immorality. All other sins a man commits are outside his body, but he who sins sexually sins against his own body
(1 Cor. 6:18).*

Flee the evil desires of youth, and pursue righteousness, faith, love and peace, along with those who call on the Lord out of a pure heart (2 Tim. 2:22).

The Backward Strategy–Satan's third strategy to keep you from pure joy and passionate living is a simple strategy that we all face. Satan reminds us of all the things we have done in the past that were a disappointment to God. He makes us feel that we aren't worthy of serving God or being loved by God because of our past sins.

That lie is totally opposite of God's grace. Jesus came so that we may have a full life. When Satan uses the backward strategy and gets us thinking about our many mistakes, we are prevented from living full, joyous lives.

During your personal quiet time, make a list in your journal of those sins that Satan continues to throw back at you. Ask the Lord to begin to cleanse your mind of these thoughts and attitudes.

Pray this prayer:
You have said in Your Word that if we confess our sins, You are faithful and just to forgive us of our sins and cleanse us of all unrighteousness. I know that You are a God who forgives and erases the sins of our past through the blood of Your Son. Therefore, I cast down and rebuke these thoughts of my failures. I realize that Satan is the accuser of the brethren, that he wants more than anything to handicap me by continually reminding me of events that occurred in my past. But I will no longer be subject to his accusations because You have cleansed my life and made me a new person. I am in You and, therefore, I am a new creation; the old has gone and the new has come. I praise You for Your incredible love that is able to take the garbage of my past and wipe the slate clean. I know that You see me as righteous through Christ. I pledge to You that I will begin a passionate pursuit of Your will, forgetting what is behind and looking forward to what is ahead because I am a new creation. In Jesus' name, Amen.

God's Promises to Overcome Satan's Backward Strategy:

"The thief comes only to steal and kill and destroy; I have come that they may have life, and have it to the full" (John 10:10).

Not that I have already obtained all this, or have already been made perfect, but I will press on to take hold of that for which Christ Jesus took hold of me. Brothers, I do not consider myself yet to have taken hold of it. But one thing I do: Forgetting what is behind and straining toward what is ahead, I press on toward the goal to win the prize for which God has called me heavenward in Christ Jesus (Phil. 3:12-14).

Yes! WHEN THE DEVIL REMINDS YOU OF YOUR PROBLEMS, YOU REMIND HIM OF HIS DEFEAT.
—GABRIEL HEYMANS

"For I will forgive their wickedness and will remember their sins no more" (Heb. 8:12).

The Mind: An Incredible Vessel

Emma's Journal

God, help me go back. I can't live like this!
These thoughts that storm inside me,
Tearing me to pieces.
Accusation,
Condemnation,
I never could.
I never will.
I am so restless. I can't sleep.
I can't imagine going on like this.

My mind keeps scanning the surface for peace.
I read the *Rolling Stone*
The peace doesn't come.
See a romantic movie
It's not there.
Listen to Blink 182
It doesn't help.
Indulge in cookies 'n cream
I starve myself
Lose ten pounds
But the thoughts remain
And the mind is still not satisfied.
There's a void
An emptiness inside me.
God, if you really do exist,
Stop these thoughts that bind me to the past
And compel me to do the same things
Over
And over
And…

Perhaps one of the greatest arguments against the concept of creation by chance is the incredible organ called the brain. There are about 100 billion neurons in the human brain, and each has about 10,000 contacts with other neurons. The neurons of one human cerebral cortex would reach over 250,000 miles if placed end-to-end.[1] Our mind was created by God to do incredible things, and it does. Just think about the great minds of this generation and how they have literally changed the face of civilization. And yet for most humans, the mind (God's incredible gift to man) has been distorted and corrupted by the satanic system that surrounds us. Our minds are constantly bombarded by strong images of sexuality, violence, hatred, disillusionment, and atheism.

What areas of purity in your own life have been attacked by information, images, and sounds of the fallen world? _____

_____

_____

_____

_____

Spend a few moments meditating on this list of satanic tools that corrupt the mind. What strategies do you find yourself confronted with on a daily basis?

___ **Sexual images on television**
___ **Internet pornography**
___ **Explicit lyrics in music**
___ **Foul language of people around you**
___ **Explicitly violent scenes in movies and television**
___ **Graphic sexual conversation on the Internet**
___ **Graphic sexual conversation and joking with friends**
___ **Pornography on pay movie channels and cable networks**
___ **Self-defeating thoughts**
___ **Seductive comments spoken to and received from others**

You were taught, with regard to your former way of life, to put off your old self, which is being corrupted by its deceitful desires; to be made new in the attitude of your minds; and to put on the new self, created to be like God in true righteousness and holiness (Eph. 4:22-23).

What other areas and choices do you confront that are danger zones and satanic tools to undermine your purity?

_____

_____

_____

Spend some time today taking inventory of the impurity you have been confronted with in the past. Read _Psalm 26_.

David wrote this psalm in celebration of a pure life. In _verse 2_ he said, _Test me, O Lord, and try me, examine my heart and my mind._ Are you willing to take the time to allow the Lord to reveal areas of impurity in your mind? Are you willing to commit, as David did in _verse 3_, to walk continually in God's truth? In this short psalm, David painted a portrait of a pure mind.

After you read this psalm, answer these questions.
Do you avoid friends who lie and are full of deceit and controversy? _____
Do you hang around people who say they are Christians, yet their lives are no different than atheists? _____
Do you love to party with _the assembly of evil-doers (v. 5)_? _____
Do you worship as David worshiped? Do you go to the altar with a pure heart? _____
Do you praise the things of this world, or do you praise God for His wonderful deeds _(v. 7)_? _____
Do you love to dwell with God, or do you hang out with friends who have evil schemes? _____

In _Psalm 26:11_, we see what God wants from us today and for the rest of the time we are given on this earth. He wants us to live a blameless life, but this blameless life is not something we can do on our own. In _verse 11_ we find the key to this blameless life. David cried out to God to redeem him and to be merciful to him. That's how David found purity in his life. It wasn't that David was a perfect man; he was far from it. But he realized that when he walked with God, he was made pure by faith.

Read _Romans 8:6_.

The mind of sinful man is death, but the mind controlled by the Spirit is life and peace (Rom. 8:6).

What is the result of a sinful man's mind? _____

What is the result of a mind controlled by the Spirit? _____

Read *Romans 12:2.*

Do not conform any longer to the pattern of this world, but be transformed by the renewing of your mind. Then you will be able to test and approve what God's will is—his good, pleasing and perfect will (Rom. 12:2).

In this passage of Scripture, we once again are confronted with a choice of the mind. What are the two choices Paul gives us?

_____

_____

_____

Read *Philippians 3:17–21.*

Join with others in following my example, brothers, and take note of those who live according to the pattern we gave you. For, as I have often told you before and now say again even with tears, many live as enemies of the cross of Christ. Their destiny is destruction, their god is their stomach, and their glory is in their shame. Their mind is on earthly things. But our citizenship is in heaven. And we eagerly await a Savior from there, the Lord Jesus Christ, who, by the power that enables him to bring everything under his control, will transform our lowly bodies so that they will be like his glorious body (Phil. 3:17-21).

LOOK!

IT'S HARD FOR GOD TO WALK WITH A MAN WHO GETS HIS MIND MADE UP TO DO THINGS HIS OWN WAY.
—NORVEL HAYES

There comes a time in the life of a follower of Christ where he has to decide whether he will live a life fully devoted to Christ or whether he will become an enemy of the cause of Christ. *Philippians 3:19* tells us what the life of an enemy contains. Paul writes, *Their destiny is destruction.* If we live in the pattern of the world, we have to come to accept that in the end, the things we lived for will all be burned. Paul continues by saying *their God is their stomach.* The enemies of the cross are not controlled by their minds. They are controlled by their base desires, their sexual desires, their desires for food, and other passions. And still Paul continues by saying their glory is in their shame.

This is a perfect description of the culture in which we live. Things that used to bring shame to people suddenly are glorified on talk shows, movies, and music videos. Therefore, we have a choice as citizens of heaven. *Set your minds on things above, not on earthly things (Col. 3:2).* We can choose to glory in things that are shameful or glory in the cross of Christ. God wants to renew our minds. He wants to change the choices we make on a daily basis. Only then will we see God move in an incredible way.

Finally brothers, whatever is true, whatever is noble, whatever is right, whatever is pure, whatever is admirable, whatever is lovely—if anything is excellent or praiseworthy—think about such things (Phil. 4:8).

Speaking of choices made on a daily basis, think about this. Would the television shows that you spend your hours absorbing be considered *true* or *noble*? Would you say that the Web sites you surf are *right* or *pure*? How *admirable* and *lovely* is your favorite soap opera?

Write the names of the shows and/or sites that you spend the most time watching/visiting. Place a check mark beside each of the adjectives from *Philippians 4:8* that could describe the show or site. Then total the number of check marks in each column.

	SHOW NAME	SHOW NAME	SITE NAME
TRUE			
NOBLE			
RIGHT			
PURE			
ADMIRABLE			
LOVELY			
EXCELLENT			
PRAISEWORTHY			
TOTALS			

Now that you are aware of what you are feeding your mind daily, be bold enough to get rid of those things that won't help you on your journey to a pure mind. This may mean actually destroying some CDs, turning off the computer, or giving relationships over to God. It may mean seeking a godly person who can walk you through the process of purity. God deeply wants you to experience the purity of your mind.

How can a young man keep his way pure? By living according to your word. I seek you with all my heart; do not let me stray from your commands. I have hidden your word in my heart that I might not sin against you (Ps. 119:9-11).

God's Word tells us the key to keeping our way pure. What is it?

_____

_____

Below are a few Scriptures for you to memorize on your way to pure joy. Take the time during this study to hide these in your heart. Add others to this list when you memorize these.

❏ *Psalm 139:23-24*   ❏ *Proverbs 4:23-27*   ❏ *Romans 12:1-2*
❏ *1 Corinthians 10:13* ❏ *Philippians 4:8* ❏ *1 Thessalonians 4:7*
❏ *James 1:12*   ❏ *1 Peter 1:15*

Pray this prayer:
Father, You have said in Your Word that You want us to come to You and to reason with You. Though our sins are like scarlet, You will make us white as snow. Father, I give to You my mind. I pray that You will give me the courage and desire to experience purity and to cast down those thoughts that are contrary to what You want to do in my life. Father, these are the things I wish to change in my life: _____

_____

_____

_____

_____

Quality

A THOROUGH KNOWLEDGE OF THE BIBLE IS WORTH MORE THAN A COLLEGE EDUCATION.
—THEODORE ROOSEVELT

Thank You, Father, for a new chance. I thank You that You do not seek to condemn me, but to bring me into a right relationship with You, a relationship that is full of joy and fulfillment. I seek Your pure joy through the blood of Jesus. Amen.

You will keep in perfect peace him whose mind is steadfast, because he trusts in you (Isa. 26:3).

THREE STEPS TO MENTAL PURITY
Step 1. Realize that there's a difference between worldly wisdom and godly wisdom.

Never before in the history of the world have there been so many educated people, yet so little wisdom. This era is a technological explosion of facts, knowledge, and discovery; yet we see dramatic increases in sexually transmitted diseases, bankruptcy, violence, and suicide. What's going on? Why can't we use all of these wonderful innovations and advances to end all the madness that surrounds us?

The answer is simple. Worldly wisdom leads to shame and death. Godly wisdom leads to a life of passionate, pure joy.

Proverbs 4:7 nails the concept, *Wisdom is supreme; therefore get wisdom. Though it cost all you have, get understanding.*

So where do we get this wisdom? That's the bottom line, isn't it? More than 4,000 years ago a man named Job asked that very question.

"Where then does wisdom come from? Where does understanding dwell? It is hidden from the eyes of every living thing, concealed even from the birds of the air. Destruction and Death say, 'Only a rumor of it has reached our ears.' God understands the way to it and he alone knows where it dwells, for he views the ends of the earth and sees everything under the heavens. When he established the force of the wind and measured out the waters, when he made a decree for the rain and a path for the thunderstorm, then he looked at wisdom and appraised it; he confirmed it and tested it" (Job 28:20-27).

Here is the answer.

And he said to man, 'The fear of the Lord—that is wisdom, and to shun evil is understanding' (Job 28:28).

But what about all the intellects who say there is no God and that this world is a by-product of chance and evolution? We have to keep in mind that intellect apart from God is dead to wisdom.

The fool says in his heart, "There is no God" (Ps. 14:1).

History proves these verses over and over:
• You can be a world leader and still be sexually perverted.
• You can have fame and riches and still be thrown into a deep depression.
• You can marry the most beautiful woman or handsome man and still be dissatisfied.
• You can be a CEO, yet end your life with total regret.
• You can be royalty and have no control over your impulses that lead to destruction.

Why do these tragedies occur? It's because the secret to success and pure joy is wisdom. God challenges you to pray the prayer that a student named Solomon prayed.

Solomon answered, "You have shown great kindness to your servant, my father David, because he was faithful to you and righteous and upright in heart. You have continued this great kindness to him and have given him a son to sit on his throne this very day. Now, O Lord my God, you have made your servant king in place of my father David. But I am only a little child and do not know how to carry out my duties. Your servant is here among the people you have chosen, a great people, too numerous to count or number. So give your servant a discerning heart to govern your people and to distinguish between right and wrong. For who is able to govern this great people of yours?" (1 Kings 3:6-9)

This student-turned-king slam-dunked it! Solomon, in his youth and inexperience, knew the secret to success. And look how God responded.

The Lord was pleased that Solomon had asked for this. So God said to him, *"Since you have asked for this and not for long life or wealth for yourself, nor have asked for the death of your enemies but for discernment in administering justice, I will do what you have asked. I will give you a wise and discerning heart, so that there will never have been anyone like you, nor will there ever be. Moreover, I will give you what you have not asked for—both riches and honor—so that in your lifetime you will have no equal among kings. And if you walk in my ways and obey my statutes and commands as David your father did, I will give you a long life"* (1 Kings 3:10-14).

Ask God to give you wisdom each day. Confess to Him that He knows what will happen this day and you don't. Ask Him to give you wisdom to live this day as He sees fit.

If any of you lacks wisdom, he should ask God, who gives generously to all without finding fault, and it will be given to him (Jas. 1:5).

Step 2. Realize that there is a battle being waged between the Holy Spirit and the prince of this world (Satan). Therefore we must take authority over destructive thoughts.

Yes! THE GREATEST BATTLES ARE FOUGHT IN THE MIND. —CASEY TREAT

The battleground is your mind. Satan's empire works around the clock to incite the thoughts and emotions of Christians. He is constantly proposing alternates, shortcuts, and slick tricks for instant, short-lived fulfillment.

If you are a normal teenager, the thoughts that come into your mind in an average week are too many to count.
• It's just a set of answers. The test is going to be too difficult. This is the only way you're going to salvage a *B*.
• You love him, and he really needs you to do this thing. He might not stick around if you don't.
• The music is so cool. Forget the lyrics; they don't matter. Go ahead, you know how much you'll enjoy having it.
• Dad laid down the law about seeing Jeff; but he doesn't think you're mature enough to handle situations alone, and you know you can. Just tell him you're going to the library.

• Is it really gossip if you know it's true? You know that Brandon has to be wondering, and he'd appreciate the info.

Be self-controlled and alert. Your enemy the devil prowls around like a roaring lion looking for someone to devour (1 Pet. 5:8).

The apostle Paul gives us direct instructions about how to deal with thoughts that come into our minds. He says:

For though we live in the world, we do not wage war as the world does. The weapons we fight with are not the weapons of the world. On the contrary, they have divine power to demolish strongholds. We demolish arguments and every pretension that sets itself up against the knowledge of God, and we take captive every thought to make it obedient to Christ (2 Cor. 10:3-5).

Our thought life is serious business. Therefore, we shouldn't allow Satan's proposals to just hang around inside our head.

How would you take the following thought captive and make it obedient to Christ? *It's just a set of answers. The test is going to be too difficult. This is the only way you're going to salvage a B.* _____

_____

_____

_____

This is what Paul is talking about when he says to take every thought captive. If your mind generates a thought that is anti-Christ in principle, you must call it what it is and nuke it! Don't even weigh the options of ungodly alternatives. Flee. To use an ancient Hebrew expression, just say to that lie, "See ya! Wouldn't wanna be ya!"

Step 3. The eyes, the flesh, and the ears are channels through which both poisons and nutrients enter the mind. You must make difficult choices to protect the health of your mind.

Slop is slop is slop is slop.

There is no second-hand use for slop. It is food for pigs. It doesn't matter if it comes in a shrink-wrapped container or if you ride in a limo to the hog pen. The slop remains slop. Are you willing to partake in things that gag the Holy Spirit? Are you willing to take an inventory of the things that you touch, hear, and see? It really comes down to a matter of belief in God. Do you believe that God is going to totally astound you with His blessing if you are fully devoted to Him? Or do you believe that if you live a pure life you'll end up becoming some bored, prudish legalist? Jesus came to save us from boring, prudish legalism and give us pure, passionate joy.

"The eye is the lamp of the body. If your eyes are good, your whole body will be full of light. But if your eyes are bad, your whole body will be full of darkness" (Matt. 6:22-23).

He said He'll fill you up and you won't be in need. (Do you believe it?) He said that He will bless you beyond measure. (Do you believe it?) He said if you stay in Him, you can ask what you will and He will do it. (Do you believe it?) He said that God is a giver of good gifts. (Do you believe it?)

If you choose to think thoughts contrary to God's plan, then you are shaking your fist at Him and saying, "I don't trust Your way. I know what's best for me. So leave me alone. I can live this life with my own ability to make choices."

Keep in mind that many people who choose this wishy-washy, on again/off again lifestyle are simply nonbelieving churchgoers. They're the ones who will cry out, "Wait a minute there, God! Didn't you see me at church? Didn't you see me singing songs and giving my testimony? Didn't you see me on the mission trips and in the musicals and in the FCA?" *Matthew 25:41* contains the verdict to these people who look religious but don't cling to and trust in God: "Leave. I never knew you."

But God's plan for His children is simple:
Get wisdom.
Identify the source of your thoughts.
Don't get muddled in the slop.

A COMMITMENT OF MY MIND

I choose to have the same mind that is in Christ Jesus and to think things that are true, noble, right, pure, lovely, admirable, excellent, and praiseworthy. I place the helmet of salvation to guard my heart and my mind. I commit to take every thought captive to the obedience of Christ. I commit to seek the wisdom that is more valuable than precious jewels.

1. "About Neurotransmission- Some Brain Facts," *Viable Herbal Solutions,* <http://www. herbal-solutions.com/health1/health74.htm> (22 May 2001).

The Emotions:
Powerful
Motivators

Jenny ran into her bedroom and slammed the door. She had tried so hard to make it through the past few days. Finally it was Friday, and the emotions wouldn't be held captive any longer. She and Jeff had dated for five months. It had seemed to be a storybook romance. She felt as if Jeff had helped her discover who she really was. She felt sure she was in love, and she had seen no end to the relationship, even though she was only a sophomore in high school.

The beautiful portrait of love had shattered before her very eyes when, out of nowhere, Jeff said he wanted to end the relationship. Before she knew it, Angela, a friend of hers since elementary school, seemed to be with Jeff all of the time. Jenny's sorrow, rage, regret, and confusion drove her to her knees that afternoon. Her emotions were real, but she had to find something stronger than her relationship with Jeff to hang onto if she was going to survive. During the past week, she had thought about revenge and even suicide. She just wanted some way to escape the circumstances that had led to her emotional storm.

Does Jenny's story sound familiar? Chances are that you or one of your friends have been through a week like Jenny's. For reasons too many to count, the teen years are filled with emotional ups and downs. Sometimes the G-forces of relationships, hormones, and the search for identity make a normal week seem like a triple-looped roller coaster. The world around you is changing fast. You are surrounded by friends who are also trying to find their place in the midst of all this social chaos. You are confronted by relationships that have the potential to be life-changing, destructive, and eternal.

So how are you, as a follower of Christ, going to deal with the emotions that you feel on a daily basis? Are these emotions somehow evil? Does

God want you to live a numb, callused life void of emotions? Does the Lord want you to sit back, hide away, and hope that these roller coasters will subside when you turn 20? Is it wrong to fall in love? These questions have an easy answer: no, on all counts. The emotional roller coaster that you are feeling as a young adult is a gift to be harnessed.

Perhaps the best term used for the emotional life of a believer is *passion*. That may not have been the word you expected to see in a book about sexual abstinence and moral purity, but let's take a look at the definition of passion. Passion is an intense, driving, or overmastering feeling; a strong devotion for some concept.[1] Christians should be the most passionate people on the face of the earth! God didn't create us to be droopy, unemotional followers, clinging only to concepts and facts and never truly experiencing the exhilaration of emotions.

Read *Psalm 63:1-8*.
What are some of the words or phrases used in this passage that reveal an attitude of passion toward God? _____

_____

_____

Students sometimes allow their emotions to be the basis of their actions. Their emotions become the engine of their lives rather than the caboose. Here are some examples of students who allow passions to control their lives:
- Kirk is so crushed after the breakup with Josie that he doesn't want to go to church because he's afraid he might see her there.
- Sarah becomes consumed with Paul to the extent that she feels insecure to participate in any activity when he is not around.
- Tanner always ends up in a yelling match with his dad when they try to talk about college choices.
- Paige thinks that Damion will notice her if she just loses 10 more pounds.
- Dana's cruel words just seem to fly out of her mouth without passing by her brain first. Especially when she is upset, she says things that hurt her friends' feelings.
- Terrance still can't believe that they got beat in overtime. Now that his football career is over without a championship, he feels like a failure, and he's too embarrassed to go to school or church.

• Michelle Lewis thinks Adam Gregory is just dreamy. Sitting in class, she doodles on her folders, *Michelle Gregory* or *Mrs. Adam Gregory,* and thinks about what their kids will look like.

Do any of these situations sound familiar to you? We all are subject to powerful emotions that can easily change our words, actions, decisions, and mission in life. God has a plan for you. It is for you to experience pure joy! Pure joy is the quiet, confident assurance and stability that come from absolute surrender to Him and His will.

What role do emotions play in your life? _____

_____

_____

Jesus told us that He came to give us overflowing, rich, abundant lives *(John 10:10).* That's what He does. If, as Christians, we are controlled by emotions, we are failing to take Jesus at His Word. We must acknowledge that emotions exist and that they are powerful motivators. They can change our entire perspective on our surroundings. But we must remember that emotions are not necessarily reality. Emotions can be deceptive and therefore are a favorite strategy of Satan.

AMAZING!

LIFE IS 10% WHAT HAPPENS TO YOU, 90% HOW YOU RESPOND TO IT.
—CHUCK SWINDOLL

MAKING IT PERSONAL
How can you keep your emotions "in check" and out of the reach of Satan's influence? _____

_____

_____

_____

As Katie's youth minister, I saw her develop from a moderately devoted follower of Christ to one of the youth group leaders. She was active in many areas of our church and seemed to be filled with joy. After an incredible experience at youth camp, she made a commitment to full-time ministry. We were stoked! What an incredible act of faith! A few weeks later, her father was diagnosed with an inoperable brain tumor. After a hard-fought 10 weeks, he died. There's no way to express the emotional torment Katie experienced. There were moments when all she could do was weep and worship. God just seemed to carry her through the experience.

A friend asked Katie if she ever got mad at God. I listened as she explained her relationship with God in a way very few people could.

"I was way beyond anger. I was mad at God for my dad's death. My prayers certainly didn't sound religious. There were times when I wish He would have taken me. But I learned that my God is bigger than my emotions. He could see through my darkness. Nothing changed about God through the summer. He remained God. And I learned that if I run to Him even in anger, He can take it. He's a big God. My dad's death didn't change the facts. He's still Father God. He still knows everything I need. He never turned His back on me, even when I wanted to turn my back on Him. He was stubbornly holding on to me. I've learned that emotions are bad decision-makers. I need to trust God and keep on walking with Him. Soon the emotions will come around."

AMAZING!

CHRIST ALONE CAN BRING LASTING PEACE—PEACE WITH GOD—PEACE AMONG MEN AND NATIONS—AND PEACE WITHIN OUR HEARTS. —BILLY GRAHAM

The lesson in a nutshell: Recognize that emotions are powerful motivators, but poor engines.

TEST YOUR EMOTIONS KNOWLEDGE
True or False?

____ 1. A sign of spiritual maturity is always feeling happy and content.

____ 2. We can make solid decisions about dating based on how we feel about someone.

____ 3. Emotional abuse can happen in a romantic relationship.

____ 4. A person can't be angry and pure at the same time.

____ 5. If someone makes you angry, you should try to avoid confrontation.

____ 6. True character is revealed during times of difficulty and disappointment.

_____ **7. Going to a counselor for help in dealing with painful emotions implies that you aren't strong enough to solve your personal problems.**

_____ **8. Expressing emotion is a sign of spiritual and personal weakness.**

Answers

1. False. We see in *Psalm 38, Psalm 55:1-5,* and again in *Psalm 56:3,8* how David was crying out to God at times when he felt less than happy and content. Read these passages and understand how David was spiritually mature at a time in his life when he was lonely, depressed, and just plain scared.

2. False. *Jeremiah 17:9* tells us that *the heart is deceitful above all things and beyond cure. Who can understand it?* Therefore, trusting our emotions and our heart to make solid decisions is not wise. Has your heart ever deceived you? God's Word is the only truth we can trust when making important decisions.

3. True. Emotions are highly volatile. With a word, they can be changed. In romantic relationships, emotions can be battered, bruised, and crushed by hurtful words or degrading attitudes. Or they can be nourished, protected, and uplifted by encouraging words and serving attitudes.

4. False. Remember Jesus at the temple? Do you think He was a little angry at the money-changers and the people buying and selling in the house of prayer? Read about it in *Matthew 21:12-13.* We know from Jesus' example that being angry doesn't discount your purity.

5. False. Jesus' teachings in *Matthew 18:15* tell us, *If your brother sins against you,* (which would probably make you angry) *go and show him his fault, just between the two of you. If he listens to you, you have won your brother over.* In the previous example of Jesus at the temple, we see that when Jesus became angry He confronted the people and told them, *"My house will be called a house of prayer, but you are making it a 'den of robbers.'"* (Matt. 21:13)

6. True. Jesus' true character was revealed in *Matthew 26:36-46* when He knew His time on earth was almost finished. We know it was a difficult time for Him because He said, *"My soul is overwhelmed with sorrow to the point of death (Matt. 26:38).* Even in this time of despair, Jesus prayed for His Father's will to be done. *"My Father, if it is not possible for this cup to be taken away unless I drink it, may your will be done." (Matt. 26:42)*

7. False. God doesn't want us to go through our tough times alone. He gives us help in friends, family, counselors, and others. *Proverbs 19:20* says, *Listen to advice and accept instruction, and in the end you will be wise.*

8. False. Many psalms written by David are full of emotion. Check out *Psalm 95:1-2* and *Psalm 100*. Can you sense the emotion he had as he wrote about God? David is regarded as a mighty warrior and a man after God's own heart, and yet he expressed his emotions and passions in songs and prose recorded throughout the Bible.

THE EMOTIONAL QUICKSAND: SATAN'S TACTIC FOR CHRISTIANS IN EMOTIONAL PAIN

Since pain is a certainty in this life, how do you plan to deal with it? That's what you must decide *before* the pain occurs. Pain is simply a tool. If pain is put into the hands of God, it can revolutionize your destiny and lead to joy. Believe it or not, pain can be a road that leads to pure joy. However, pain in the hands of Satan can absolutely shred your destiny.

Read *Hebrews 12:2*. How did Jesus deal with the pain? _____

_____

_____

_____

_____

_____

The apostle Paul is an example of a Christian who experienced pure joy in times of pain. *I consider that our present sufferings are not worth comparing with the glory that will be revealed in us (Rom. 8:18).*

He announces his discovery that, as Christians, our crosses will always lead to empty tombs, our wounds will lead to crowns, and our suffering is a bargain-basement price for the ecstasy of heaven. I wish that books could be printed with flashing neon arrows, because I would have them pointing at that verse. What we suffer *is not even worth sharing space on a page* with the description of what our eternity will be like and the glory (passionate joy) that is revealed in us!

SATAN'S QUICKSAND PROCESS
Phase 1: Up to Your Knees! Malice and Resentment

Sadly, pain usually produces resentment. It's our natural instinct to want to blame some*one* or some*thing* for the pain. It's a much easier route to take because it doesn't take any faith to look for someone to blame. However, it does takes faith to believe that God will use a tragedy or painful event to draw you into a deeper relationship with Him.

Imagine this: *As you walk through the hall of your school on your way to your locker, you notice people staring at you strangely, as if something is out of place. Snide remarks, giggles, and whispers follow you all the way to your locker. When you finally reach your locker, it all makes sense. Someone has written on your locker with a thick, red marker. The writing contains several vulgar slams about you and your physical appearance.*

What is your reaction? _____

_____

_____

Believe it or not, this could be your finest hour. This might be the chance for you to show your classmates a portrait of Jesus that they've never seen before. No one can say that it won't hurt.

Resentment comes when we are violated and we begin to look for ways to hurt back. It might not be displayed immediately because we can store up resentment. We drop the joy of the cross and pick up a burden of malice. Malice says, *I'll never forgive.*

Phase 2: Wading in the Sludge! Peer Identification

If resentment and malice move into your room along with their infamous buddies preoccupation, revenge, and profanity, you'll find that they don't like to be alone. The progression continues. If we have resentment toward someone, our flesh will begin to hunger for others who resent.

Here's a simple example. Mrs. Perkins, your science teacher is obviously unfair in her grading. You put 110 percent effort into your projects and reports, but she never gives you anything higher than a *B-*. On top of that, she is constantly making jokes about "narrow-minded Christians" and their fairy-tale beliefs. Then there's Ted. Ted is obviously her favorite student. She talks to him after class every day, always laughs at his jokes, and gives him high grades. Last week his grade was the same as yours, even though the project he turned in was two days late!

Who would you first go to when you want to express your anger? Place a check mark by your answer.
❑ **Ted, the obvious golden boy of the class.**
❑ **Malia, a girl who also is furious with Perkins for other reasons.**

Our sin nature draws us like a magnet to other people who resent. Birds of a feather really *do* flock together. Peer identification is why sexually active people hang out with other sexually active people. It's why students who get smashed out of their wits on vodka and ecstasy hang out together. This is such an important key to pure joy because the people you hang out with during your high school and college years will shape your destiny.

He who walks with the wise grows wise, but a companion of fools suffers harm (Prov. 13:20).

Phase 3: Neck High! Sensual Indulgence
What happens when hurting people who have chosen the path of resentment group together? They find ways to kill the pain by acting on their emotions. We almost always connect the word *sensuality* with sexual sin, but sensuality is a much broader concept. It is feeding the senses, emotions, and flesh without accounting for logic and your spiritual condition. Sensual indulgence is the stuff that feels good when you do it; but when the indulgence is over, the emptiness and lack of joy is even greater than before. Listed below are some examples of sensual indulgence.

• Responding to lust through extended times of kissing and petting.
• Responding to frustration or loneliness with a pint of premium, rocky road ice cream.
• Responding to anger with your parents by cranking up the volume of your music.
• Responding to sadness and grief by drinking alcohol with friends.
• Responding to rebellious feelings toward society with vandalism.

Phase 4: Fighting for Your Next Breath! Accusation and Shame
Satan wants to lead us into shame after we indulge in sensual, spiritless actions. He is so hypocritical! First he tempts us, and then he accuses us for giving in to the temptation. That is why he bears the names Accuser *(Rev. 12:10)*, Liar *(1 John 2:22,2; John 1:7)*, Thief *(John 10:10)*, and Prostitute *(Rev. 17:1)*.

Examples of this pattern flow freely from God's Word. From the beginning of world history, this pattern was in motion.

Resentment: Adam and Eve began to question and resent the law of God.
Peer Identification: They began conversing with someone else who questioned God's authority: Satan.
Sensuality: They decided to do what they thought would feed their flesh. They ate the forbidden fruit.
Shame: They hid from God.

We see the same pattern repeated in the lives of people throughout Scripture. Fill in the blanks with the name of the person who fell into Satan's destructive pattern.

The first murderer, _____. (See *Gen. 4:1-16*.)
A man consumed with lust to the point of seeing someone killed, _____. (See *2 Sam. 11*.)
The betrayer, _____. (See *Matt. 26:14-56*.)
God's muscular servant who lost it all because of lust, _____. (See *Judg. 16*.)
The man who tried to run away from God's plan, _____. (See *Jonah 1*.)
The men who sought to kill Jesus, _____. (See *Matt. 26:1-5*.)
A man whose rage and jealousy ultimately cost him the throne and his life, _____. (See *1 Sam. 18, 19, 31*.)

Some of these biographies have triumphant endings. There were those who recognized their wickedness and repented. Others were tragically cursed as simple tales of caution. It's as if God's Word underscores this spiritual concept and warns us of the impact of an emotional landslide.

MAKING IT PERSONAL
What emotional pain are you experiencing today? _____

_____

_____

How are you choosing to deal with the pain? _____

_____

_____

God doesn't desire for us to be slaves to our emotions, living on a roller coaster of emotional ups and downs, twists and turns. God didn't intend for us to take hairpin curves and emotional free-falls, continually repeating the cycle, never going anywhere in particular.

As Christians we must base our lifestyle on the consistent road of God's Word, not the rocky, ever-changing path of emotions. Emotions are a gift from God. Without them, we couldn't function as He intended. The Lord loves a passionate heart! Throughout history He has used people who were passionate about the cross of Christ to change the world.

The people that God uses and chooses, God's all-stars, are not people of ability; they are people of availability who have learned the secret of giving their praise to God. If you use your life for the glory of God, God will use your life for His glory. –James Merritt

A COMMITMENT OF MY EMOTIONS
I commit my emotions to God. I cast my cares upon Him, knowing that He cares for me. I turn away from those emotionally toxic attitudes that cause me to lose focus; and I seek to become an imitator of the Lord. I will welcome God's plan for my life with the joy given by the Holy Spirit. I choose to trust His Word more than my emotions, knowing that He cherishes my feelings and seeks to deliver me from the curse of sin to the joyous blessing of His eternal kingdom.

1. Merriam Webster's Collegiate Dictionary, 10th ed., s.v. "passion."

The Spirit: Being Possessed by God

The issue of spiritual purity is confusing to most Christians. It's widely ignored because the purity of spirit isn't something that you can see with your eyes.

If you're like most Christians, you spend your time trying to change your actions and behaviors. These outward elements could be considered the fruit of your life. You've got good fruit and you've got bad fruit. But you can't change the fruit without addressing the roots. How odd for a farmer to expect oranges from a tree with roots that are from an oak!

For the sinful nature desires what is contrary to the Spirit, and the Spirit what is contrary to the sinful nature. They are in conflict with each other, so that you do not do what you want....But the fruit of the Spirit is love, joy, peace, patience, kindness, goodness, faithfulness, gentleness and self-control. Against such things there is no law (Gal. 5:17, 22-23).

So what's the secret to eliminating the bad fruit in your life? There is no secret, complex formula. You simply have to address the inner motives and the causes of the sin.

Read *2 Corinthians 10:4*.
The weapons we fight with are not the weapons of the world. On the contrary, they have divine power to demolish strongholds (2 Cor. 10:4).

What are our weapons? (See *Eph. 6:10-18* for help.)

_____

_____

These spiritual strongholds have roots that need to be completely eliminated for us to experience freedom and purity as we follow Christ. To understand the importance of spiritual purity, you first have to grasp the biblical facts of spiritual warfare and strongholds.

"Innumerable strongholds are connected to an unwillingness to forgive. Left untreated, unforgiveness becomes spiritual cancer. Bitterness takes root, and since the root feeds the rest of the tree, every branch of our lives and every fruit on each limb ultimately becomes poisoned. Beloved sister or brother, the bottom line is … unforgiveness makes us sick. Always spiritually. Often emotionally. And, surprisingly often, physically."[1]

Yes! YOU MAY AS WELL QUIT READING AND HEARING THE WORD OF GOD, AND GIVE IT TO THE DEVIL, IF YOU DO NOT DESIRE TO LIVE ACCORDING TO IT. —MARTIN LUTHER

Dear friends, do not believe every spirit, but test the spirits to see whether they are from God, because many false prophets have gone out into the world. This is how you can recognize the Spirit of God: Every spirit that acknowledges that Jesus Christ has come in the flesh is from God, but every spirit that does not acknowledge Jesus is not from God (1 John 4:1-3).

The following process is perhaps the most important part of the journey toward purity. You can try your hardest to control your mind's thought processes, your physical urges, and your emotional well-being, yet never experience victory because there remains a hook in you spiritually.

A few years ago, police in Texas were startled to find blood in a man's house after he was reported missing from work for several days. The police searched his house and discovered the blood smeared on the floor leading into a closet. There they found the corpse of the man who had apparently been strangled to death by his pet boa constrictor. As the story goes, the victim and the snake had been faithful companions since the snake was only two feet long. The man prided himself in feeding the animal every time he ate a meal. Evidently the snake grew tired of the arrangement one day; and while curling itself around its master, it began to do what its name implies! It began to constrict its body, squeezing the oxygen out of the man's lungs. The blood that the police found smeared on the floor was blood from the snake as the victim tried to stab the snake in desperation.

This story, as told by Dr. Ken Hemphill, is a perfect parallel of what a stronghold does when we allow it into our spirit and then feed it. It will continue to grow like any healthy pet. And the more we feed it, the bigger it will get, until one day this spiritual snake will begin to rear its ugly head and contract its body, bent on destroying our mission and life in Christ.

Here are five of the many spiritual strongholds that might find a home in your heart.

A SPIRIT OF JEALOUSY
Jealousy is a primary tool Satan uses to keep you from spiritual purity. If you remember, jealousy is one of the first sins recorded in the Bible. Cain and Abel, sons of Adam and Eve, experienced the curse of jealousy. Cain, being controlled by jealousy, became the first convicted murderer of the human race. It's interesting also to note that the jealousy erupted over worship issues.

Read *Genesis 4:3-8*.

The root of jealousy produces a variety of bad fruit including murder, revenge, spite, rage, hatred, cruelty, rivalry, envy, and divisions. When we allow a place in our spirit for jealousy, we open our lives up to Satan's influences.

Read *1 Samuel 18*.

LOOK!

AND OFT, MY JEALOUSY SHAPES FAULTS THAT ARE NOT.
—WILLIAM SHAKESPEARE

We see a king anointed by God who allowed jealousy to destroy him as a leader. When the young David defeated Goliath, all of Israel praised and celebrated David's victory—all but King Saul. David was just a kid in Saul's eyes, and yet the boy received such praise that it was too much for King Saul to take. In *verse 6,* Saul's sudden demise begins.

When the men were returning home after David had killed the Philistine, the women came out from all the towns of Israel to meet King Saul with singing and dancing, with joyful songs and with tambourines and lutes. As they danced, they sang: "Saul has slain his thousands, and David his tens of thousands." Saul was very angry; this refrain galled him. "They have credited David with tens of thousands," he thought, "but me with only thousands. What more can he get but the kingdom?" And from that time on Saul kept a jealous eye on David (1 Sam. 18:6-9).

The Scripture records that an evil spirit tormented Saul and ultimately made him so angry that he attempted to murder David.

MAKING IT PERSONAL
Have you allowed a spirit of jealousy to reside in your life? ____
Have you been jealous of your siblings? ____
Have you ever been jealous of a person who had a relationship with someone you wanted to date? ____
Have you nurtured a spirit of jealousy because of money or someone else's accomplishments? ____

Record in your journal an inventory of your life. Identify where you see the spirit of jealousy and ask the Lord to release you from its dangerous grasp.

A LYING SPIRIT
Read *Psalm 31:18*.
Let their lying lips be silenced, for with pride and contempt they speak arrogantly against the righteous (Ps. 31:18).

LOOK!

> I HAVE HELD MANY THINGS IN MY HANDS, AND I HAVE LOST THEM ALL; BUT WHATEVER I HAVE PLACED IN GOD'S HANDS, THAT I STILL POSSESS.
> —CORRIE TEN BOOM

In this passage, David leads us to the root of the lying spirit. This spirit of deception is something we face on a daily basis. The lying spirit can take on many forms. Listed below are some of those forms and extra spaces for you to add your own.

• Flattery • Gossip • Excuses
• Deceptive Lifestyles • Accusations
• Slander _____ _____

TO TELL THE TRUTH

Have you made statements that were untrue to get on the good side of a friend or teacher? _____

Have you made a habit of lying to your parents? _____

Have you gossiped and lied about your peers in order to seek subtle revenge? _____

Have you lied about your spiritual relationship with Christ in order to appear righteous before others? _____

Spend a few moments in prayer asking the Lord to reveal to you areas in your life where you have not lived a life of truth. Pray this prayer for truth:

Yes! *A LITTLE LIE IS LIKE A LITTLE PREGNANCY. IT DOESN'T TAKE LONG BEFORE EVERYONE KNOWS.*
—C. S. LEWIS

Father, You told us that we would know the truth and the truth would set us free. I accept the spirit of truth into my life. I rebuke (cast down, kick out, forbid it to remain) any deceptive operation or way of speaking that has gained access to my life. By the blood of Christ, I refuse the evil path of deception. I choose to follow You in truth. In Jesus' name and by His shed blood, Amen.

A SPIRIT OF PERVERSION

Perversion is simply living out a life that is the opposite of a godly lifestyle.

- God tells us that we should believe in Him with all our heart.
  A perverse spirit says that God doesn't exist.
- God tells us that life is precious and that we should value life.
  A perverse spirit tells us that life is a choice and that suicide and abortion are legitimate options.
- God says that we should expose ourselves to things that are pure and holy.
  A perverse spirit attracts us to thoughts and imaginations that are tainted.
- God says that sex is a wonderful gift to be shared in a marriage relationship—one man, one woman.
  A perverse spirit distorts sex and creates homosexuality, pornography, sexual abuse, incest, bestiality, and countless other perversions.

MAKING IT PERSONAL

Spend a few moments alone and think about your life. Ask the Lord to reveal those areas in your life when a perverse spirit has confronted your mind.

Do you find yourself drawn to programs, movies, and talk shows that glorify sex before marriage, homosexuality, or bisexuality? _____

Have you been lured into pornography, Web sites, stories, emotions, and sounds that excite you sexually? _____

Do you have a desire to seduce or manipulate the person you date or with whom you associate? _____

Have you allowed worry to dominate your thought process? _____

Do you find yourself seeking human answers without asking God for guidance? _____

Meditate on these questions and patiently wait for God to reveal areas in your life where Satan has been allowed to plant the seeds of perversion. As you make a list of these things in your journal, use this prayer as a guideline for pulling up the roots of perversion in your life.

Father, I thank You for the cross of Christ. I thank You that His sacrifice gives me victory over any spirit of perversion. I ask You through the blood of Jesus to purify my heart. I cast off these perverse spirits that have warred against my intimacy with You.

Confess each sin or satanic strategy that the Holy Spirit pointed out to you during your time of meditation.

1. _____
2. _____
3. _____
4. _____
5. _____

I repent and turn away from these things, and I declare independence and freedom in my life. Thank You for offering complete forgiveness. Teach me to walk in the way that is right. In Jesus' name, Amen.

A SPIRIT OF PRIDE

Pride is a favorite tool of Satan when he's dealing with us. It would be impossible to list the ways pride manifests itself. Gigabytes of documents couldn't recount all of Satan's victories when he has used this spirit against the church.

AMAZING!

SOME NEVER GET STARTED ON THEIR DESTINY COURSE BECAUSE THEY CANNOT HUMBLE THEMSELVES TO LEARN, GROW, AND CHANGE. —CASEY TRENT

People who let the spirit of pride into their lives carry a spiritual arrogance. They react in a smug way toward people they feel are inferior to them. They criticize people whom they believe are wrong. A person with pride may angrily scorn his parents or friends. She may be stubborn and unwilling to change. The spirit of pride will cause us to reject our desperate need for God and fellow Christians.

It's impossible to ignore the path of destruction that is caused by pride when we study the Bible. In *Daniel 5:20* we read about the pride of King Nebuchadnezzar.

But when his heart became arrogant and hardened with pride, he was deposed from his royal throne and stripped of his glory (Dan. 5:20).

In the Bible we find other examples of the effects of pride. See *2 Chronicles 26:16; Psalm 10:4; Proverbs 8:13;* and *Proverbs 11:2.*

Have you ever been a servant to others and experienced freedom from the spirit of pride? If you have, write about your experience. _____

_____

_____

When you are serving someone, can you still have a spirit of pride? Explain. _____

_____

_____

_____

_____

What areas of your life have been overtaken by pride? Ask the Lord to begin to transform your life into a story of humble service. Pray this prayer:

Lord Jesus, You should be my example of living in humility. Even though You had power beyond anything we can imagine, You humbled Yourself and became a servant. Lord, I wish to follow You into a life of humility. Throughout Your Word it is obvious that pride hardens the heart. I'm asking You to break me and soften my heart so that I can be like You. I rebuke this stronghold of pride that has found a place in my heart. I don't want to live as a proud, religious person. I want to be like You. Thank You for breaking the chains of pride in my life. In Jesus' name, Amen.

A SPIRIT OF BONDAGE (ADDICTION)

Don't you know that when you offer yourselves to someone to obey him as slaves, you are slaves to the one whom you obey—whether you are slaves to sin, which leads to death, or to obedience, which leads to righteousness? (Rom. 6:16)

Why do young people fall victim to addiction? _____

_____

_____

_____

_____

_____

List addictions that are holding you or your friends captive. ____

_____

_____

_____

_____

_____

Whenever you experience a lack of peace, Satan is on the spot to offer alternatives. When these alternatives become habitual activity, they will lead the Christian into bondage. Ask the Lord for insight into areas of your life where you have allowed Satan access to create addiction and spiritual bondage.

Place a check mark beside any words on our list of addictive strongholds that you didn't write on your list above.

❏ **Drugs**   ❏ **Alcohol** ❏ **Pornography** ❏ **Cigarettes**
❏ **Eating Disorders**❏ **Television** ❏ **Internet**   ❏ **Adrenaline***
❏ **Rage**   ❏ **Romance**   *an addiction to excitement

To experience pure joy, we must rely on nothing else but Christ to satisfy our souls. Ask the Holy Spirit to reveal any addictive chains in your own life.

In your journal, write the areas of addiction that you need Christ's help to overcome. Start planning for success by writing specific goals of how you are going to rely on God's peace and say no to Satan's alternatives. Write out your prayer in your journal.

A SPIRIT OF WITCHCRAFT

Before you immediately skip this section, please realize that most witchcraft in our society is not found when the moon is full and the black cloaks are handed out! The spirit of witchcraft is found in all areas of our culture. It's a stronghold that infiltrates the media and our social relationships.

In *Acts 16:16-18,* we read about one encounter that Paul and Silas had with witchcraft.

Once when we were going to the place of prayer, we were met by a slave girl who had a spirit by which she predicted the future. She earned a great deal of money for her owners by fortune-telling. This girl followed Paul and the rest of us, shouting, "These men are servants of the Most High God, who are telling you the way to be saved." She kept this up for many days. Finally Paul became so troubled that he turned around and said to the spirit, "In the name of Jesus Christ I command you to come out of her!" At that moment the spirit left her (Acts 16:16-18).

Perhaps the greatest danger for Christians as they confront evil is to believe that satanism and witchcraft are imaginary and that they have no power in the real world. We are in a spiritual battle where evil spirits fight against the Holy Spirit. Satan, the master of deceit, disguises witchcraft as things we think of as "just a game" or "merely a story."

When we adopt that attitude, his plan of making his ways a normal part of our everyday life is succeeding. Here's a short list of Satan's ways that we are getting used to seeing every day:

• Fortune-telling
• Astrology
• Horoscopes
• Magic
• Ouija boards
• Psychic phenomenon
• Occultic music
• Dark games
• Spells, chants
• Necromancers (supposedly speaking to the dead)
• Icon worship
• Eastern spiritual arts

MAKING IT PERSONAL
Spend a few moments asking the Holy Spirit to remind you of times when you've allowed Satan to influence your life through a spirit of witchcraft. The Lord wants you to rebuke (to cast out in the name of Jesus) these spiritual forces. Don't allow them to get a foot in the door.

The strongholds we have studied in this chapter are just five of the many that God calls us to cast out of our lives. Don't procrastinate in dealing with these issues. Search your life and allow God to heal you from spiritual strongholds and restore you with a pure spirit so that you can live the joy of the Christian life. If you simply choose to ignore spiritual strongholds, they will continue to hold you in bondage and silently destroy your spiritual walk with Christ. Don't hesitate to see a counselor or minister if you are struggling with these issues. You might want to find someone in your church that could help walk you through the process of spiritual purity.

A COMMITMENT OF MY SPIRIT

I realize that my struggle is not against flesh and blood, but against the rulers, against the authorities, against the powers of this dark world, and against the spiritual forces of evil in the heavenly realms. I receive the Holy Spirit and ask Him to baptize and cleanse me from all spiritual wickedness. I commit to be a soldier in the warfare of grace and not a spectator in the warfare of religion. I cast down those things that would so easily entangle me so that I can worship God purely in spirit and truth.

Quality

HE WHO KNEELS THE MOST STANDS BEST.
—D. L. MOODY

1. Beth Moore, *Praying God's Word* (Nashville: Broadman and Holman Publishers, 2001), 220.

The Body: A Temple Worth Protecting

You would never guess that Kerry was an abused girl at Western High. It seemed, on the outside, that she had everything in its place. She was constantly on the go, trying to accomplish as much as she possibly could. But inside she knew that she was teetering on the edge of disaster. She wondered why she felt so tense. She never seemed to have any joy, even though her whole life seemed charmed.

Kerry's journal entry, April 6.
Today was another confusing, fast-paced, and totally unfulfilling day. I feel like my entire life is enslaved by an impossible schedule. I just don't seem to have the energy that I used to have. I used to love going to school and seeing my friends; but lately I have been edgy, stressed out, and more than a little nervous about whether I can keep up this pace. Some days I'm so depressed that I don't think I can take another step forward, yet there's no time to slow down. Is this the way all Christians feel? God, where is the peace You promised? Instead of that serene feeling that I thought You'd give me, my heart races, my nerves are at the breaking point, my eating habits are horrible, I only sleep about five hours at night, and I feel like everything is closing in on me. Lord, show me what to do. I'm at a total loss.

Kerry's feelings are not unusual. She is simply one more voice crying out from the body of Christ for peace and rest. Somewhere along the line she swallowed the idea that Christianity is simply a spiritual and mental state of being. This is a concept that just doesn't make sense. Our lives involve more than our thoughts, feelings, and emotions. God gave us an incredible temple. It's a temple worth protecting.

How do the following Scriptures describe your body?
1 Corinthians 6:19 _____

_____

Matthew 26:41 _____

_____

Proverbs 14:30 _____

_____

A mysterious truth is found in *2 Corinthians 4:10*. Paul describes to the church of Corinth that, as Christians, we carry around in our body the death of Jesus so that the life of Jesus may also be revealed in our body. In other words, we are containers of Christ Himself. On the opposite end of the spectrum, Satan realizes that if he can shorten our life or weaken the health of our body, he can ultimately destroy the effectiveness of our mission on earth.

The greatest single cause of atheism in the world today is Christians who acknowledge Jesus with their lips, then walk out the door and deny Him by their lifestyle. That is what an unbelieving world simply finds unbelievable. −Brennan Manning

FIVE THREATS TO PURE JOY IN THE BODY

Threat 1: A Restless Lifestyle
It's a fact that people are working more these days than they ever have in the history of the world. It may not be physical labor, but the inability to unplug from the stresses of activity and the inability to get proper amounts of sleep on a consistent basis threaten our existence in numerous ways. Believe it or not, God is not in the business of freaking you out. He doesn't want you to be so exhausted and burned out that you're useless to the ultimate mission of His kingdom.

Check the following statement that would best describe your life.
❏ **I'm constantly moving from one promise to the next.**
❏ **I try to carve out at least five hours of sleep at night.**
❏ **So many invitations, so little time.**
❏ **I feel that God is most pleased when I am very busy.**

❑ I make rest a priority because it is a spiritual act.
❑ I rarely have time to do things with excellence.
❑ I feel like a firefighter rushing from one crisis to the next.
❑ I see people as a mass of walking, breathing needs and
   problems that only I can correct.

I believe that one of the primary messages Jesus has for young Christians is simply this: *Slow down; do fewer things; strive for excellence, not quantity. I long to spend time with you in silence. Busyness seems to be a false god. Allow Me the opportunity to radically change the content of your life.*

The Hit List: Make a list of activities you could eliminate to create a simpler lifestyle. _____

_____

_____

Threat 2: A Passive Lifestyle

Cal is certainly not in the minority. He's just another junior trying to succeed academically. He doesn't take amphetamines or sedatives, he doesn't smoke pot or cigarettes, he never drinks or risks life and limb by imitating the stunts he sees on the X-Games. But there is something lacking in his life. He seems to be nervous and unfulfilled. He often naps during class or after school. At night he lays in bed hoping to get enough sleep, but his mind just doesn't quit. When he becomes anxious he retreats to the computer to escape from the day-to-day madness.

So what's the secret sin? Cal is a mouse potato, constantly in front of the computer. He rarely goes outside after he gets home from school. His body doesn't get the exercise that it needs. God created the body to run, lift, and play. If we aren't getting the physical activity that we need, it will be very difficult to avoid the stresses of life.

MAKING IT PERSONAL
Over the past seven days, what physical activities have you done in order to keep your temple vibrant and healthy? _____

_____

_____

_____

JAKE'S WAY-COOL CAR

Imagine that Jake, on the eve of his 17th birthday, was given an incredible, new car. With a sleek design, a powerful engine, and the works, the car was engineered to be driven. But Jake's favorite thing about the car was the CD player, with a 12-disc changer and a powered subwoofer. He really didn't want to drive it at all. However, as you know, a radio doesn't keep the engine healthy. It's simply there for entertainment and information. Using the radio and never turning on the ignition will ultimately run down the battery.

Isn't that the way we are whenever we fail to use our bodies in physical exercise? Remember, if your car gets sick and it's not working to your satisfaction, you can always trade it in for a newer model. Not so with your body. You get one engine, one transmission, and one chance to take care of it. The owner's manual suggests daily maintenance. Once you've trashed it, it's a major pit stop for you. (Besides, part replacement is really expensive.) It's important to train God's temple and to exercise your Christ-container called the human body.

Pure Joy Challenge: Would you be willing to commit your body to the Lord, making a part of that commitment an effort to exercise three days a week for at least 20 minutes? _____

MAKING IT PERSONAL
Create a plan that works for you. Keep in mind that your body needs a Sabbath, a day of rest. That's a part of the equation. Important note: If you fall out of the habit, don't beat yourself up over it. Just get back to your commitment as soon as possible.

By making this commitment, chances are you'll be extending your life span and, therefore, expanding your ministry and passion as a Christian.

Threat 3: Eating Disorders
Abby woke up thinking about food and how to avoid it. She prided herself in her discipline. It thrilled her when friends commented on how thin she was becoming; she loved the attention it brought her. She would pat herself on the back because of the weight she had lost, but the next second she was back to worrying about getting to exercise that evening. All throughout the day she thought of strategies of avoiding food.

Lately, she had been thinking about how she was going to cover up her obsession at the school awards banquet. She knew it was going to be a potluck dinner, and she cringed at the thought of all the fatty casseroles and fried chicken. To get her mind off the banquet, she tried on her new size-two dress to make sure it still fit.

Abby was nominated for several awards and was expected to take home some of the highest honors. Calling her a perfectionist would be an understatement. She made straight A's, was involved in all the big clubs, and was even a cheerleader. Teachers often commented on how mature she was for a teenager.

Her prayers lately had become requests for God to strengthen her willpower and deliver her from food temptations. She also had to pray for physical stamina many times as she felt light-headed during cheerleading practice. Ever since the youth minister's wife had approached her about getting too thin, Abby had felt uncomfortable going to church. Abby agreed to talk to her but then tried to stay away for a while. At school and at home, she wasn't bothered by anyone wanting to *help* her. They all complimented her or ignored her. She was safe in those places.

In addition to losing some weight, Abby noticed other things happening to her body. Her once thick, curly, brown hair gradually started breaking and thinning. Along with the stomach cramps came dark circles under her eyes and yellowing skin. She couldn't understand why she was cold all the time. But in her obsession to be thin, none of these ailments would stop her. She looked at them as things she would have to live with … maybe die with.

On the day of the awards banquet, Abby wanted to squeeze in a few minutes of exercise before it was time to go. She had an eerie feeling just thinking about being in the same room with all that food. After about 10 minutes on the treadmill, her muscles felt tingly; and then everything went dark. She woke up in a hospital with tubes and machines connected to her body. Her mom was in the corner of the room, crying.

Abby's story is much like that of the typical sufferer of anorexia nervosa, but eating disorders take many different forms and can happen to anyone. Eating disorders damage more than your body; your emotions and mind suffer harm as well. Eating disorders are about so much more than food, which makes understanding them so difficult.

"In trying to understand the causes of eating disorders, scientists have studied the personalities, genetics, environments, and biochemistry of people with these illnesses. As is often the case, the more that is learned, the more complex the roots of eating disorders appear."[1]

God created you with a need to be fulfilled, to be satisfied. He wants to be the One who fulfills your soul and satisfies your life. When an eating disorder encompasses your being, you are trying to replace God with a false sense of fulfillment and satisfaction. That is why eating disorders destroy. They can not and will not take God's place.

The presence of an eating disorder in your life can crowd out the joy Jesus wants to give. It can take over your life. Every thought and every action becomes a slave to the disorder. Whether anorexia, bulimia, or compulsive overeating, the disorder has control over you.

If you suffer from an eating disorder, have you given control of your life to God? If you haven't, pray something like this:
Lord, You are my Creator and my Sustainer. I really want to find my satisfaction in You. Please remove these lies in my head that are constantly telling me that I'm not good enough. They are destroying my spirit and my body. I know my body is Your Holy Spirit's temple. Forgive me for treating it so poorly. Help me to honor my body in all I do. Lord, it is so hard for me to change my ways, but I rely on Your strength to help me. I give control of my life to You. In Jesus' name, Amen.

Do you believe He has the power to overcome your disorder? ___

Do you trust Him to deliver you from your eating disorder? ___

Now to him who is able to do immeasurable more than all we ask or imagine, according to his power that is at work within us (Eph. 3:20).

Eating disorders have varying effects on the body. Many cases have even led to death. Listed below are some physical effects of eating disorders.[2]

ANOREXIA
- irregular heartbeat, cardiac arrest, death
- kidney damage
- liver damage
- destruction of teeth
- rupture of esophagus
- disruption of menstrual cycle, infertility
- weakened immune system
- icy hands and feet
- swollen glands in neck
- excess hair on face, arms, body
- dry, yellow skin
- anemia
- fainting spells
- permanent loss of bone mass
- brittle nails and hair

BULIMIA
- rupture of esophagus
- heart failure
- destruction of teeth
- fatigue
- brittle nails and hair
- others common to anorexia

OVEREATING
- high cholesterol
- high blood pressure
- diabetes
- other obesity problems

THE WORLD TELLS US
Beauty is on the outside.

GOD TELLS US
Beauty is on the inside.

Your beauty should not come from outward adornment, such as braided hair and the wearing of gold jewelry and fine clothes. Instead, it should be that of your inner self, the unfading beauty of a gentle and quiet spirit, which is of great worth in God's sight (1 Pet. 3:3-4).

THE WORLD TELLS US
Fat isn't accepted.

GOD TELLS US
I accept and love you.

The Lord does not look at the things man looks at. Man looks at the outward appearance, but the Lord looks at the heart (1 Sam. 16:7b).

THE WORLD TELLS US
Only the weak need help.

GOD TELLS US
I want to help you.

"Come to me, all you who are weary and burdened, and I will give you rest" (Matt. 11:28).

THE WORLD TELLS US	GOD TELLS US
It's your body; do what you want.	**Your body is Mine.**

You are not your own; you were bought at a price. Therefore honor God with your body (1 Cor. 6:19-20).

Threat 4: The Low-Down on Getting High

We all know that using drugs and alcohol won't enhance your life, even though hundreds of thousands of students use them on a daily basis.

No one says, "Hey, I think I'll start pumping these chemicals into my body so that I can waste all of my money and suffer physical side effects like loss of memory, brain damage, accidents, impotence, hair loss, blood-shot eyes, uncontrollable bladder function, and frequent vomiting. I might even get to lose all my self-esteem, future vocational opportunities, and friends. What a deal!"

SPECIAL YOUR HEAVENLY FATHER IS TOO GOOD TO BE UNKIND AND TOO WISE TO MAKE MISTAKES. —CHARLES H. SPURGEON

You're probably surrounded by people who use some kind of drug, whether it's alcohol, nicotine, amphetamines, sedatives, or designer drugs such as ecstasy. Students are drawn to experience drug usage when they are trying to fill a void of dissatisfaction and a desperate need to kill the pain brought on by the circumstances of life. The bottom line is that a drug user has not allowed Jesus to take control of the needs, wants, and hurts of his life and circumstances.

It is important to recognize drug use as a problem that finds its roots in the spirit. If your spirit is not at peace, chances of defeating the desire for drugs and alcohol are small. That's why it is important to commit to a drug-free lifestyle. Perhaps you have friends who are users, or maybe you just suspect that they're users. God may have placed you in a friend's life to help him confront his problems and defeat a potentially fatal event from occurring. Below are some signs that will provide clues.

• Expressions of low self-worth
• A sudden drop in grades
• Violent outbursts
• Sudden weight loss
• The discovery of drug paraphernalia

- Stealing or borrowing money
- Apathy
- The lack of enthusiasm about the future
- Lying and deception
- Hostility toward friends
- Glassy eyes

For you as a Christian, it's a choice of how you choose to meet your needs—emotionally, psychologically, and spiritually. In *Ephesians 5:18*, Paul presents the Christian alternative for the drug lifestyle. He says, *Do not get drunk on wine, which leads to debauchery. Instead, be filled with the Spirit.* It's obvious that if you are allowing the Holy Spirit to dominate every aspect of your life, taking drugs, getting stoned, or getting wasted on alcohol is an absurdity. If you take hold of the passionate, exciting life that the Lord offers, you are in no danger of being drawn into a web of drug use and escapism.

MAKING IT PERSONAL
What are some ways you can let others know that you choose to be filled with the Spirit rather than to be filled with drugs or alcohol? _____
_____
_____

What choices can you make today that will help you avoid drug and alcohol use in the future? _____
_____
_____

Threat 5: Premarital Sex
Is premarital sex harmful to your physical body? It's obvious that sex outside of marriage, meaning intercourse or other sex acts, is extremely damaging to your spirit, your emotions, and your mind. Now we are discovering more reasons from a health standpoint to avoid premarital sexual activity. The recent outbreaks of syphilis in junior high and high schools, along with the incredible spread of AIDS, form just the tip of the iceberg. However, this isn't something that has developed in recent history. The Bible refers to sexual sins as physically dangerous. Paul in *1 Corinthians 6:18* speaks God's Word to the early church. *Flee from*

sexual immorality, all other sins a man commits are outside his body, but he who sins sexually sins against his own body. If you are involved sexually with someone outside a marriage relationship, you're opening yourself to experience the destruction of your own body.

Let's take a look at *Hosea 8:7* where Hosea prophesied God's Word. *They sow the wind and reap the whirlwind.* What does that have to do with sexual sin? _____

_____

_____

It means that if we walk the tightrope of premarital sex, then the social, emotional, mental, and even physical consequences will be our master. There's perhaps no better illustration of this concept than the tragic story of Kevin, not his real name.

Kevin was an active member of a community church in a large city. There was really nothing deviant about his lifestyle from outward appearances. He was active in a Tuesday-night Bible study. He went to youth camp every year. He tried his best to develop a Christlike lifestyle, yet he became fixated on sexual material and cyclical, addictive sexual thoughts. He told me in counseling, "I don't know how it all started. I had been exposed to some pornography that I found in a garbage dumpster in the third grade, but it wasn't a case of me actually seeking any sort of sexual gratification on my own. I was very frustrated with the two dating relationships I had in my first two years of high school, and that seemed to just feed the compulsion that I had for an even greater sexual experience. I found myself prowling around for some way to relieve the sexual tension, and in my freshman year of college I gave in to the pressure of it all with three visits to a prostitute. I couldn't believe it when I went for a physical and was told that I had AIDS. It was like my life ended at that moment. Those words just bounced around in my head and I kept saying to myself, *No! this isn't the way my life should play out!* But I couldn't escape the truth. I gambled my life for a few moments of pleasure, and now I have to face the consequence."

Yes!

THE DESIRE OF LOVE IS TO GIVE. THE DESIRE OF LUST IS TO GET. —ED COLE

His life ended as a standing testimony of God's redeeming power; but I can't help but think of all the years he could have served God, raised a family, lived a successful, passionate life. He was extremely talented and creative. He had all the makings of a corporate CEO, and yet his life was cut short by the curse of this sin against his own body. He sowed the wind and he reaped the whirlwind.

Sexual impurity doesn't always resemble Kevin's lifestyle. Many teenagers feel that they are staying pure as long as they don't have intercourse. However, other sexual acts, also known as outercourse, are sins against your body and can have harmful physical effects. Many sexually transmitted diseases can be transmitted through oral sex and genital contact, as well as intercourse. Nearly two-thirds of all STDs occur in people younger than 25.[3]

In your journal, write the sexual sins in your life. Pray right now, asking for God's forgiveness, then for His help to avoid any other sexual sin. You can commit today to remain sexually abstinent until marriage, one way to keep your body pure.

Yes! *THE FAITH-FILLED LIFE IS DIFFICULT BECAUSE IT FORCES US TO CONTROL OUR THOUGHTS AND DISCIPLINE OUR BODIES. —CASEY TREAT*

It all comes down to this: God did not create you to be an enemy of your own body. Your body is an incredible tool of organs, tissue, cells, and systems, which God has entrusted to you for these years that you have on earth. It's not the kind of body that you will have in heaven, when you receive your new body. *But our citizenship is in heaven. And we eagerly await a Savior from there, the Lord Jesus Christ, who by the power that enables him to bring everything under his control, will transform our lowly bodies so that they will be like his glorious body (Phil. 3:20-21).* The body you have now is your responsibility. You need to treat it as a miraculous gift from God.

A COMMITMENT OF MY BODY

I acknowledge that my body is a temple of the Holy Spirit. My body is meant to bring glory to God. I commit to keep my body pure of abuse, sins of the flesh, and fatigue. I commit to get proper rest, exercise, and nourishment. I present my body as a living sacrifice, holy and pleasing to God. Because I can do all things through Christ who strengthens me, I give this vessel to God, my Heavenly Father.

1.<http://www.room42.com/store/health_center/diet_nutrition/eating_disorders.shtml #eat4> 7 Nov. 2000.
2. <http://www.anred.com> "Medical and psychological complications" 31 May 2001
3. <http://www.niaid.nih.gov/factsheets/stdinfo.htm> "An Introduction to Sexually Transmitted Diseases" 6 June 2001.

The Stand:
The Ecstasy of
Holiness

Note: If you are going through this study individually or as a group, this session is best experienced in one period of time. We believe that if you set aside at least one hour to go through this process, God will supernaturally bring you into a deeper, more intimate relationship with Him. In many ways, this experience is a worship section. It pours together all the aspects of purity that we've explored over the past five sessions. The ultimate goal is supernatural purification.

Throughout this process we hope that you've grasped that purity and passion are intertwined. In the light of Jesus' passionate grace, He is willing to meet every need that you have. He can take your life—whoever you are, whatever you've done, or wherever you've been—touch you, transform you, and make you over.

That's worth repeating. It could be the one sentence that breathes life and hope into your being.

Jesus can take your life—whoever you are, whatever you've done, or wherever you've been—touch you, transform you, and make you over.

AMAZING!

AND AS MEN ARE TRANSFORMED, THE COURSE OF A NATION CAN BE CHANGED. —WELLINGTON BOONE

As you've gone through the *Pure Joy* experience, you may have said, "There's absolutely no way I can ever reach the state of purity presented in this book." Guess what? You are correct. You can't... on your own. Holiness is a work of God, not man. But it takes a person who is willing to say, "I give up! I'm tired of trying to live the Christian life on my own!"

When you reach that point of surrender, you've crossed the threshold from people stuff to God stuff. God needs to see your white flag of surrender waving. In *Isaiah 6* we see a vision of a man who chose to stop playing church and encountered a holy, pure, incredible God. When he experienced God in all His holiness and glory, Isaiah cried out: *"Woe to me!" I cried. "I am ruined! For I am a man of unclean lips, and I live among a people of unclean lips, and my eyes have seen the King, the Lord Almighty" (Isa. 6:5).*

STEP 1: UNDERSTAND WHERE YOU ARE. TAKE A LOOK AT THE FATHER.

Journal entry:
*In the year of disappointment, loneliness, fear... In the year of confusion, desperation and chaos. I saw the Lord. My eyes had been blinded by amusement, toys, wealth, dreams, and aspirations. In the midst of the sandcastles of my own self-importance, my eyes were blinded by the temporal until an eternal God shook the foundation of my soul. He came to me and I saw myself for who I was outside of Him: spiritually naked, dying, cold, starving, and helpless. He came to me at a time when my hopes were dashed, when my future appeared bankrupt. He came to me when every solid foundation seemed to collapse. He came to me in the poverty of my own understanding. He came to me! With a quick fix? No. With a list of seminars and books to read? No. He came to me and there was nothing, absolutely nothing, I could offer in my own strength. The masks, alibis, and diplomas faded under the light of His passionate gaze. I didn't have the answers. For the first time in my life I knew that no word, no thought, no event would change me. Only God. **Christ alone** could change my heart. He came to me. He wrapped His arms around me and said, "My beloved, I've been waiting for you."*

LOOK!
GOD IS NOT MOVED OR IMPRESSED WITH OUR WORSHIP UNTIL OUR HEARTS ARE MOVED AND IMPRESSED BY HIM.
—KELLY SPARKS

Once we wave the white flag of surrender, God is free to work.

Read *Psalm 85:9*.

What is the attitude of a God-possessed student? _____

_____

_____

Pray this prayer:
Lord I see You in Your glory and power. I can never reach the standard of purity that You want me to reach. It is impossible outside of Your supernatural work in me. Father, I see myself as I am.

Using your spiritual journal or the space below, write a description of your spiritual state. This is between you and God. Be honest. _____

_____

_____

_____

_____

STEP 2: UNDERSTAND WHERE YOU NEED TO BE. UNDERSTAND GOD'S DESIRE.

Through the course of this process, you've read about where you need to be to experience pure joy. Do you remember Jesus' words that He spoke to the lost generation of that day?

"Come to me, all you who are weary and burdened, and I will give you rest. Take my yoke upon you and learn from me, for I am gentle and humble in heart, and you will find rest for your souls. For my yoke is easy and my burden is light" (Matt. 11:28-30).

Jesus' offer still stands.

If you have never reached out to Him, be assured that He's reaching out to you. He's saying, "Come." If you are weary, come. If you are tired of the hurried pace, the performance-based lifestyle of the world, come. Jesus loves you unconditionally, which is hard for us to accept when we live in a world of terms, fine print, loopholes, and exceptions. He is offering you the greatest gift you could ever receive. He loves you so much that He ignored the consequences in order to bring you into a right relationship with God. What's the catch? The catch is that you can't earn your way into an eternal relationship with Him. He simply asks you to drop all your tools, coping mechanisms, and survival strategies and come. That's it. You may have lived your entire life going to church, yet for the first time all the pieces are coming together.

If you are ready to enter into this incredible relationship, pray something like this prayer right now:
Lord Jesus, I am tired of trying to live my life by myself. I'm tired of trying to measure up to worldly standards and expectations. I'm stopping all my self-saving attempts because I realize that my only hope is You. I believe in You. I turn away from life outside Your grace. I accept Your forgiveness and eternal life.

We've all been called names from time to time. It's a universal experience. What names have you been called?

Lazy	Genius	Stupid
Failure	Capable	Helpless
Wise	Strong	Weak
Popular	Geek	Depressed
Attractive	Ugly	Immature
Rebel	Freak	Insane
Hyper	Sickly	Courageous
Fearful	Consistent	Friendly

God has a plan and a name for us. **Check out *Isaiah 62:4.***
No longer will they call you Deserted, or name your land Desolate. But you will be called Hephzibah, and your land Beulah; for the Lord will take delight in you (Isa. 62:4).

There are lots of strange names in this passage. The point that the Lord is making to His family is that He has a different name for us. The world might have discounted you or slapped a painful label on your life. It just doesn't matter!

Your *new* name is "righteous." It's not a name that you deserve. You can never earn it. That's why it's called *grace*. You simply receive it, and through God's power, you begin the journey of becoming exactly what your name implies.

MAKING IT PERSONAL

In the space below or in your spiritual journal, list the things that you've discovered about your actions over the past sessions of *Pure Joy*. *Example: I've discovered that I have been often jealous of my closest friends and it has been a hard, daily struggle.*

_____

_____

_____

_____

_____

_____

_____

STEP 3: ASK FOR GOD'S REVELATION. SEE WHY YOU LIVE LIKE YOU DO.

This is not a question of outward appearances. This is a matter of the heart. God's revelation cuts through all the images and acts of behavior to spotlight why you live like you do.

This process of spiritual cleansing is a must if you want deliverance from the cycle of sin that keeps you from experiencing pure joy. Only God's work of revealing why you are defeated by the sin will empower you to overcome it. Just as successful sports teams study the films of their opponents, we must study Satan's unique game plan and have a strategy for victory.

He reveals deep and hidden things; he knows what lies in darkness, and light (Dan. 2:22).

"Teach me, and I will be quiet; show me where I have been wrong" (Job 6:24).

At that time Jesus said, "I praise you, Father, Lord of heaven and earth, because you have hidden these things from the wise and learned, and revealed them to little children" (Matt. 11:25).

In silence ask God for those deeper answers to why you have a certain sin which enslaves you.

You might pray, *Lord, You know that I fall into damaging cycles of lust and guilt. Why do I act this way? Reveal the hidden things in my spirit. I confess that I'm clueless about many of my impulses. I need You to reveal these hidden things so that I may be healed.*

God might speak, *You struggle with lust because you are lonely and it is a way to help you mask the pain. Trust in Me to heal you.*

Use the following table or your spiritual journal as a guide to discovering the root of your sin patterns.

	FRUIT	**ROOT**
Example:	*Lust*	*Loneliness*

STEP 4: CONFESS TO GOD YOUR SIN, SHORTCOMINGS, HARD-HEARTEDNESS, AND FEAR, TOGETHER WITH YOUR GROUP AND INDIVIDUALLY.

Example: *Lord, I confess this fear of rejection that has driven me to drink at parties and to go too far physically on dates. This fear is something that I must turn over to You because I can't overcome the weight of it on my own.*

Read the following Scriptures and take time alone to journal and to confess the roots of iniquity that you need God to drive out, through the blood covenant of Jesus.

I confess my iniquity; I am troubled by my sin (Ps. 38:18).

If we confess our sins, he is faithful and just and will forgive us our sins and purify us from all unrighteousness (1 John 1:9).

Against you, you only, have I sinned and done what is evil in your sight, so that you are proved right when you speak and justified when you judge (Ps. 51:4).

STEP 5: CAST DOWN STRONGHOLDS.

As you discovered in the session on spiritual purity, it is impossible to gain a victory over impurity until you understand that these things aren't just simple, face-value problems. These strongholds are a part of Satan's larger conspiracy to destroy you. You can't achieve victory until you discover whom you are fighting.

Review these Scriptures and then confess these strongholds for what they are. Cast them down.

LOOK!

HAVE YOU PRAYED ABOUT YOUR PROBLEM AS MUCH AS YOU HAVE TALKED ABOUT IT? —JAMES CARNAGHI

The weapons we fight with are not the weapons of the world. On the contrary, they have divine power to demolish strongholds. We demolish arguments and every pretension that sets itself up against the knowledge of God, and we take captive every thought to make it obedient to Christ (2 Cor. 10:4-5).

Then I heard a loud voice in heaven say: "Now have come the salvation and the power and the kingdom of our God, and the authority of his Christ. For the accuser of our brothers, who accuses them before our God day and night, has been hurled down" (Rev. 12:10).

Example prayer: *Lord, through the power of Christ's blood, I rebuke and cast down these strongholds that have been created to destroy me. I no longer give credibility and allegiance to these tactics. I praise You that You came that I could have life and have it fully, and victoriously. Whom shall I fear? You are greater than this stronghold. I declare before You and before the world that You, Lord, are all I need.*

STEP 6: RELEASE FORGIVENESS.

"And when you stand praying, if you hold anything against anyone, forgive him, so that your Father in heaven may forgive you your sins" (Mark 11:25).

There's no getting around it. There's no loophole or excuse for unforgiveness in our lives. If we choose not to forgive, we will not be forgiven.

Unless you open yourself to release forgiveness, you can't open yourself to receive forgiveness.

There are many students reading this book who have been hurting for years. Maybe you are one of those. You think you are over it, and then it all comes back again. Pay close attention. God wants to heal you. But the only way you are going to receive forgiveness is by offering forgiveness.

In your spiritual journal, use the following prayer as a guide as many times as necessary, with as many names as necessary so that you can be purified from the sin of unforgiveness.

Lord, I forgive _____
This person (or group) hurt me by _____
_____
_____
_____
_____

I release forgiveness and choose to release past resentment and hurt that I have experienced regarding them. I pray that you, Lord, will begin to heal me of the pain, through the blood covenant that You established on the cross.

STEP 7: RECEIVE FORGIVENESS.

Read God's promise to us found in *Hebrews 10:16-23*.

"This is the covenant I will make with them after that time, says the Lord. I will put my laws in their hearts, and I will write them on their minds."

SPECIAL
BE QUICK TO REPENT AND QUICK TO FORGIVE AND YOU'LL NEVER BE FAR FROM GOD.
—KENNETH HAGIN

Then he adds: "Their sins and lawless acts I will remember no more." And where these have been forgiven, there is no longer any sacrifice for sin. Therefore, brothers, since we have confidence to enter the Most Holy Place by the blood of Jesus, by a new and living way opened for us through the curtain, that is, his body, and since we have a great priest over the house of God, let us draw near to God with a sincere heart in full assurance of faith, having our hearts sprinkled to cleanse us from a guilty conscience and having our bodies washed with pure water. Let us hold unswervingly to the hope we profess, for he who promised is faithful (Heb. 10:16-23).

Quality

REPENTANCE IS A CHANGE OF WILLING, OF FEELING, AND OF LIVING, IN RESPECT TO GOD.
—CHARLES FINNEY

We have to acknowledge that only through the blood of Jesus Christ can we overcome the strategy of Satan.

They overcame him (Satan) by the blood of the Lamb and by the word of their testimony; and they did not love their lives so much as to shrink from death (Rev. 12:11).

STEP 8: CELEBRATE WITH THE HIGH PRAISES OF WORSHIP.

Give thanks. If you have sincerely worked through the process of *Pure Joy,* you experienced the miracle of God's grace. It's worthy of your worship.

Let the high praises of God be in their mouth, and a two-edged sword in their hand (Ps. 149:6, KJV).

Write your own praise to God. It can be a song, a poem, or just words of thanksgiving and praise. _____

_____

_____

_____

_____

David speaks of the high praises of God in *Psalm 149:6* as a praise that is radical praise. God's work of redemption and forgiveness gives birth to full vocal, emotional, and transformational worship of the Lord. This kind of praise allows the worshiper to simply focus on God. For some this might mean kneeling. For others, it might mean simply closing their eyes and blocking out all distractions. Still, for others, it might mean other expressions of worship. Feel free to be yourself and give your worship to God.

STEP 9: TELL SOMEONE. (ACCOUNTABILITY)

Finally, find one or two friends of the same sex as yourself. Meet weekly with these friends to be accountable to each other. This is what the body of Christ is all about, holy dependency on each other. In James' letter, he tells us that being accountable to each other in the area of sins and shortcomings is a part of the healing process.

Therefore confess your sins to each other and pray for each other so that you may be healed. The prayer of a righteous man is powerful and effective (Jas. 5:16).

Solomon underscores that going solo is not the best plan when it comes to surviving times of warfare. In *Ecclesiastes 4:9-12*, he writes:

Two are better than one, because they have a good return for their work: If one falls down, his friend can help him up. But pity the man who falls and has no one to help him up! Also, if two lie down together, they will keep warm. But how can one keep warm alone? Though one may be overpowered, two can defend themselves. A cord of three strands is not quickly broken.

List the names of two or three friends you will be accountable to on a weekly basis. _____

_____

_____

STEP 10: CAPTURE A NEW VISION AS AN INDIVIDUAL AND IN YOUR GROUP.

Read the following passages of Scripture together with your group. Spend some time discovering God's plan for the group and His plan for you as an individual.
Acts 26:16-18 (Paul's Commission)
Isaiah 6:8
Joel 2:28
Jeremiah 33:3
Jeremiah 31:13
Psalm 143:8

God has brought you through the process of purity and repentance for a greater work. He didn't just want you to be clean, He has called you to join Him on an incredible adventure. Please don't miss it.

SPECIAL

FULFILLMENT OF YOUR DESTINY DOES NOT COME IN A MOMENT, A MONTH, OR A YEAR, BUT OVER A LIFETIME. —CASEY TREAT

I'm inclined to free my mind!

It's the cerebral way to spring-fresh living! Removes the static cling of impure thoughts!

A COMMITMENT OF MY MIND: I choose to have the same mind that is in Christ Jesus and to think things that are true, noble, right, pure, lovely, admirable, excellent, and praiseworthy. I place the helmet of salvation to guard my heart and my mind. I commit to take every thought captive to the obedience of Christ. I commit to seek the wisdom that is more valuable than precious jewels.

9 780633 019655

✂ CLIP & SAVE

Guilt-free & fun all in one!

The original formula for passionate living! No more ring around the eyelids!

A COMMITMENT OF MY EMOTIONS: I commit my emotions to God. I cast my cares upon Him, knowing that He cares for me. I turn away from those emotionally toxic attitudes that cause me to lose focus and I seek to become an imitator of the Lord. I will welcome God's plan for my life with the joy given by the Holy Spirit. I choose to trust His Word more than my emotions, knowing that He cherishes my feelings and seeks to deliver me from the curse of sin to the joyous blessing of His eternal kingdom.

9 780633 019655

CHRISTIAN: The mind is still a terrible thing to waste. It is acceptable to change your mind. Any other use or rebroadcast of this material without the expressed written consent of Lucifer is strictly encouraged. A pure mind contains Scripture, worship, and the courage to be different. A pure mind contains Ten essential Commandments, which if combined with the fruit of the Spirit, create a well-balance diet. In other words, city dwellers: Feed yo mind wit da good stuff. This coupon is void in most parts of VH1, MTV, and Hollywood. All formulas are non-carnal, non-conventional, and extra-safe. Please refer to the Holy Bible for proper results. Pure Mind is a part of the Pure Joy experience. Graphic images may cause stupidity, loss of self-respect, and in rare cases, death. Please present commitment coupon to the Lord and enjoy this mind-altering lifestyle. Dry mouth is caused by the lack of moisture in one's mouth. Ninety-nine out of 100 pastors recommend Pure Mind. So who was the one nutty pastor? Rev. Steven Collins of "7th Heaven" could not be reached for comment. His publicist simply stated, "He's not a pastor. He just plays one on TV."

www.truelovewaits.com

CLIP & SAVE

CHRISTIAN: This commitment is possible if redeemed through the power of Christ. Any other use constitutes fraud and may be punishable by frustration, anxiety, and a major bummed-out existence. It is valid in the United States as well as all countries of earth. Void on Mars, Venus, and certain parts of Saturn. All formulas are non-carnal, non-conventional, and extra-safe. Please refer to the Holy Bible for proper results. Avoid absurdly sad flicks pertaining to lost loves and teenage angst, or starring Brad Pitt and sick puppy dogs. (The commitment to Pure Emotions is void on trial sizes. You really just need to commit and trust God. Don't put God to the test. Matthew 4:7.) Please present commitment coupon to the Lord and avoid stupid tax. Commitment can be made for one (1) life. You can't make this commitment for someone else. Does anybody ever read the fine print on these coupons anyway? If you are reading this you are either bored or highly inclined to detail. And if you are reading this, email us at truelovewaits@lifeway.com. Living an emotionally pure life will NOT lead to water retention, nausea, sudden silliness, lack of memory, headaches, excessive moaning, inclinations to enjoying Southern gospel quartets or Regis Philbin, or loss of appetite.

www.truelovewaits.com

A better way to feel fresh & clean!

Brimstone-free formula!

A COMMITMENT OF MY SPIRIT: I realize that my struggle is not against flesh and blood, but against the rulers, against the authorities, against the powers of this dark world, and against the spiritual forces of evil in the heavenly realms. I receive the Holy Spirit and ask Him to baptize and cleanse me from all spiritual wickedness. I commit to be a soldier in the warfare of grace and not a spectator in the warfare of religion. I cast down those things that would so easily entangle me so that I can worship God purely in spirit and truth.

9 780633 019655

✂ CLIP & SAVE

God's love has you covered.

Your body... it's a temple without the stained glass windows and the velvet foam pew pads!

A COMMITMENT OF MY BODY: I acknowledge that my body is a temple of the Holy Spirit. My body is meant to bring glory to God. I commit to keep my body pure of abuse, sins of the flesh, and fatigue. I commit to get proper rest, exercise, and nourishment. I present my body as a living sacrifice, holy and pleasing to God. Because I can do all things through Christ who strengthens me, I give this vessel to God, my Heavenly Father.

9 780633 019655

CHRISTIAN: Spiritual purity works best when combined with the active ingredients of prayer (daily) and accountability. Don't settle for cheap substitutes. They will steal, kill, and destroy! This commitment should NOT be taken with Marilyn Manson, Buddha, Psychics, Dionetics, or any other derivative products of The Bottomless Pit Inc. (Rev. 20:3). This product is Holy Spirit-enhanced and features an eternal guarantee. See your pastor for details.

www.truelovewaits.com

- -

CHRISTIAN: Purity of the body is proof of redemption. Coupon and commitment only valid when student has submitted his or her body as a living a sacrifice to God. Funny bones are real, and when they are hit, they aren't funny. For successful health and purity of the body, avoid the following: sharp objects, tight clothing, flaming hoops, the Snake River Canyon, pit bulls, rusty knives, the Oakland Raiders, vehicles traveling at a high rate of speed, artificial sweeteners, asbestos, double-dog dares, cliff-diving competitions, New York cabs, the shark-infested waters of the Great Barrier Reef, eating futons, swimming with giant squid, judging Miss Teen World pageants, cycling on ice, jay walking, grinding on stadium handrails, sleeping on escalators, consuming entire jumbo-size bags of hot cheese curls, tobacco, chicken fried steak with cream gravy, spring breaks located within a 500-mile radius of Panama City Beach, Fla., sci-fi movie marathons, and back-stage passes to NSYNC concerts. When tempted to corrupt your body, scream, "No way! End of discussion!" After this outburst, if psychotherapy is offered, decline. Visit the Pure Mind™ web site at... What? We don't have our own Web site? OK. Then visit us at www.truelovewaits.com. This commitment is valid for any size body. Before beginning any exercise program consult a physician.

www.truelovewaits.com

LEADER'S GUIDE

So you've ordered the book, you've thumbed through the pages, and you are wondering how you are going to communicate these concepts in a group setting! Don't panic. To our knowledge, no student has ever died of boredom in a group study about sex, purity, and lifestyle choices. You will have a group of students that will be interested in the topic (even though they might fake boredom from time to time.) Likewise, no adult has ever died of embarrassment from teaching this subject. So fear not. Allow God to use you and you'll be amazed by how well you'll do.

The secret to a successful presentation of *Pure Joy* is to keep the experience relevant and multisensory. Passing these truths on to them is imperative. You'll find that the leader's guide will save you a lot of time, brain drain, and expense.

Encourage the students to keep a journal of what God is doing in their lives through *Pure Joy.* They may want to just keep the journal at home as they go through the spiritual inventories and journal activities. But if you do encourage them to bring the journals to the session, ask students to refrain from reading other students' journals because the material they'll be asked to write about is pretty personal stuff.

Always begin and end the session with prayer. Pray for these things:
• Honesty among students, leaders, and God;
• Spiritual renewal and revival that follows purification;
• Sensitivity for every need, hurt, and challenge represented;
• Wisdom and spiritual insight.

Don't forget to pray as you prepare. You'll find several prayers in this book. Use these prayers and Scripture promises to intercede for students. It's a tragedy that we spend so much time planning and relating to students in ministry, but do not devote much time to pray on their behalf.

Be prepared to counsel students. Some students will have third-degree emotional burns. Pray; be ready; and, as always, don't counsel a student of the opposite sex. It's just not a good idea. If a student of the opposite sex comes to you needing to talk, graciously guide them to another adult of the same sex.

Finally, keep in mind as you teach *Pure Joy* that one of your best allies is a good sense of humor. Humor disarms students and sometimes provokes deeper discussion. Students might say things that will seem awkward and humorous, but if they see you laughing at yourself, they'll be less embarrassed by their own verbal slips and "do-overs."

The students will need to read the chapter material before each group meeting. The exception here would be the first week, when they will have just received the book. At the first group session, ask the students to read and complete the first two chapters. This will be easy for them since they'll do a lot of the first chapter during the first group meeting.

SESSION ONE

Things You'll Need
❑ music
❑ a student prepared to share a testimony about idols
❑ marker board or poster
❑ marker

Play contemporary Christian music for the students' arrival. Begin on time by asking students to briefly introduce themselves and then to complete this statement: *One day I experienced pure joy when....* The students will probably ask what you mean by *pure joy*. Tell them that right now it can mean whatever they want it to mean.

Divide the students into three or four groups and invite them to develop a commercial for a product called *Pure Joy*. It could be a detergent, food additive, a new car, or any other product that someone could buy. Give them five to seven minutes to develop it and then allow time for the groups to perform their commercials.

Now shift gears by reading from page 5 the list of reasons why Satan wants to keep them from this study.

Lead them in the Prayer of Beginning (p. 6).

Ask a leader or student to read the monologue on the next page.

Monologue

What's that? (Listening) You think I could make my peace with God? You think I could have joy? You see, that's the problem. How do you do that? And even if God does exist, do you think He'd have time to deal with a 17-year-old alcoholic? It's not like I've got a lot to offer Him. I guess I was afraid that if I found God, He would be like my father.

You know the Lord's Prayer, "Our Father who art in Heaven"? I'd get a sick feeling in the pit of my stomach when I'd pray those words. So I just stopped praying—praying anything at all.

My shrink says that that's the whole problem. I've been trying to live my life so that my dad would accept me, even now. He's been dead for two years and a couple months; but when I'm in that place between awake and asleep, I still dream that he sees me and smiles. The only thing that I see in the light of day is that strange, numb look—the emptiness behind the eyes that let me know how painful I was to behold.

Why is that? He lived in silence with me after mom left us. It was a crazy childhood. He didn't abuse me. He didn't scream or yell or ridicule. He ignored me. He was always looking for something that would erase the memory of my mom. Maybe it's because I was his last reminder of her. He just looked past my eyes—speaking only facts, avoiding any embrace.

I could blame him for my addictions.
I could blame him for my depression.
I could blame him for my emptiness.

But what good would that do now? Maybe it's true. Maybe we are just lost souls on the way to an early, desperate grave. Do you believe that? What's the big deal about church? Is it just another club? I've seen the inside of too many clubs. Is it a way to numb the pain? I've been down that road, too. Is it a way to find something else to feel guilty about? I'd never survive.

Will there be an answer? Hope? Grace? I'm at the end of the road. I'm tired of the fight. I just need to be new. That's the only reason I'd come— if I had a chance, one precious chance, to be whole.

Ask, **How would you react if you met someone who had the courage to be that honest about his or her life?**

Invite the students to spread out to find a private place where they can answer the personal questions found on pages 10-11.

Before the session, ask a student to be prepared to share about a time when she put something in place of God to the point that it became an idol. At this time in the group session, allow the student to share her experience. Alternative: Ask an adult to share, or give an example from your own life. This incident might be something very small.

On a marker board or poster, write the words *happiness* and *joy*. Explain the difference between the two concepts (see p. 13). Ask students to tell you things that make them happy, and write those under the word *happiness*. Then write the things that give them joy under the word *joy*.

Discuss Satan's Three-Pronged Strategy to steal our joy (pp. 13-18).

End the session by challenging the students to read through the first two chapters and to journal their responses to the interactive material. Remind them that this experience is a process more than it is just another class. Challenge them to make this process a priority in their life.

SESSION TWO

Things You'll Need
❏ note cards
❏ candy
❏ tall glass or cup
❏ ice cream scoop
❏ cup of motor oil

Begin with prayer. Ask God to show your group how to purify your minds and draw you into a deeper relationship with Him.

Divide the group into teams of equal numbers. Give each group a stack of blank note cards. Say: **We're going have a contest. Each team is**

to write things that they've heard and seen this week. These should be things that have simply entered your mind. (Examples: music, conversations, books, TV shows, ball games, plays, class reports.) Ask a student from each group to present his or her team's list out loud to the other groups. The team with the most items is the winner. Reward the winning team with candy.

Ask for volunteers to read *Colossians 3:17, Proverbs 4:23,* and *1 John 2:16.* Ask, **What do these verses have to do with the lists you completed a few minutes ago?**

Ask the students to look at the list of satanic tools listed on page 20. Ask: **Which of these are easily accessible to students today? What other things are danger zones around you everyday?**

Have a student read *Philippians 3:17-21.* Share with the students the process of becoming more like citizens of heaven.

Ask several students to each read one of the verses referenced on page 24. After each (if you have time) discuss with the group the relevance of the Scripture in the 21st century world.

Ask three adult leaders or older youth to briefly present the Steps to Mental Purity (pp. 25-29). Ask each one to put their step on a poster and make their point quickly and creatively.
 Optional Illustration: Ask the students, **Who would like a home-made chocolate shake?** Invite a student who raises his hand to come up to the front. Pretend like you are going to make a shake by setting out the tall glass and ice cream scoop. Before you begin, pull out a cup of motor oil. Tell the volunteer that first he needs to add this special ingredient to his shake. Ask the student, **Will you still want the shake after you put a little motor oil in it?** Explain that we should be that discriminating with the things we put in our minds. Just a little amount of impurity can make something undesirable.

Discuss their evaluations of TV shows and Web sites on their charts (p. 23), and explain that the more check marks a show or site receives, the better it is for their minds. Offer students the opportunity to contact an adult of the same sex for any counseling or discussion of this material.

Ask the students to turn to the last page of the session, A Commitment of My Mind (p. 30). Have a volunteer read this statement. Challenge the students to commit to a renewed mind, which ultimately leads to pure joy.

Invite students to clip the coupon for Pure Mind on page 75. Encourage them to place it in their Bible or on their mirror as a reminder of their quest for purity of the mind.

End the session by asking the students and adults to pray with you. Pray for the commitments the students made this week. Ask the students to spend a few moments in silent prayer and then leave the room quietly.

SESSION THREE

Things You'll Need
❏ marker board or poster
❏ marker
❏ a copy of Test Your Emotions Knowledge (pp. 34-35) for each student
❏ three students prepared to act out the Emotional Quicksand scenes
❏ an adult prepared to give a testimony about wasted emotions

As the students enter, stage an argument between a leader and a student. Example: The adult claims that the student squirted shaving cream all over his car a couple of nights before, and the student strongly denies it. After everyone's attention is turned to the argument, the group leader stops the argument and explains that it was all a set-up. Ask the students, **How did it feel to observe a fiery disagreement between two people you know?**

Ask: **How do you handle conflict? Are you a "Stuffer" (someone who holds emotions inside and never confronts)? Are you a "Spewer" (someone who lets out emotions on the person closest to him or her)?**

Ask the students to define *passion*. Write their definitions on a marker board or poster. After they've exhausted the question ask, **Now which of these defining words would be found in a passionate Christian?** Circle those words or phrases and discuss.

Ask a student to read Jenny's story on page 31. Designate discussion groups and give each group these questions: How would you deal with the difficult emotions that Jenny is experiencing? Is Jenny weak because she feels these hurts so deeply?

While the small groups remain together, read *Psalm 63:1-8*.

Hand out a copy of Test Your Emotions Knowledge (p. 34). As students complete the test, emphasize that this is simply for the sake of discussion, not to see if they've done work in the book. After they complete the quiz, spend time discussing the answers. Refer to the Scriptures given in the answers on pages 35-36.

EMOTIONAL QUICKSAND

A few days before this session ask three students to help you by developing the following situational improvisation based on the concept of emotional quicksand. Introduce each scene with exposition about the situation and how it progresses through the process.

Phase 1: Up to Your Knees! Malice and Resentment—Kristina overhears a conversation between two guys making plans to go to a school party. One guy says that Kevin—Kristina's boyfriend who had asked for a little space to figure out the relationship—is going with a friend of hers to the party.

Phase 2: Wading in the Sludge! Peer Identification—Kristina calls the school gossip queen, who then blows the story even further out of proportion.

Phase 3: Neck High! Sensual Indulgence—Kristina confronts Kevin by his locker, yelling at him, and then makes a pass at one of Kevin's friends just to get back at him.

Phase 4: Fighting for Your Next Breath!—Kristina realizes that she has gotten bad information and she calls up Kevin to apologize. He won't talk to her and hangs up. Her mom comes into her room and Kristina shouts at her mom to leave her alone.

Recruit an adult leader before the session to share about a time in his or her teenage years when he or she wasted emotions on a relationship that seems so minor today. Have the adult share his or her testimony and answer any questions.

Ask the students to turn to the last page of the session, A Commitment of My Emotions (p. 40). Have a volunteer read this statement. Challenge the students to commit to emotional purity, which ultimately leads to pure joy. Emphasize that God wants to give His children a strong emotional foundation that will make each one able to withstand even the most difficult circumstances.

Invite students to clip the coupon for Pure Emotions on page 75. Encourage them to place it in their Bible or on their mirror as a reminder of their quest for purity of the mind.

SESSION FOUR

Things You'll Need
❏ large arrows cut from construction paper
❏ tape
❏ three copies of The Report (p. 87)
❏ two copies of the Biblical Illustration (p. 88)
❏ quality time in prayer for this experience

Begin with a brief worship experience. Sing a few choruses. Ask a couple of students or leaders to lead in prayers of thanksgiving and worship.

Ask students to read A Commitment of My Spirit (p. 51). Ask, **Is it easy to make that kind of commitment?**

After the worship time, form small groups (six students maximum) with at least one adult leader in each group. Give the leaders several arrows cut from construction paper.

Read *Ephesians 6:11-18*. Ask the groups to think of the enemies in the 21st century and write each concept on an arrow. (Examples: Gangsta Rap, *Playboy*, ecstacy drugs) Let the groups tape their arrows on a focal wall. Discuss with the group the concept of spiritual armor and its importance in the fight.

Arrange for three students to read dramatically the script on the next page.

THE REPORT

Two demons enter into the office of Satan.

Demon 1: The report is in, Master! You will love the data. The strategy is working.

Demon 2: How wise you are!

Demon 1: Attacking the foe at the very heart. How brave, how scandalous, how *(laughing)* unpredictable you are, Master.

Satan: Read me the report at once!

Demon 1: Now keep in mind, these are the church kids. Sunday School kids, mind you. Those who have grown up in the church. Those who have been on the very threshold of the churches' teaching.

Demon 2: Sunday School.

Demon 1: Youth Camp.

Demon 2: Bible Studies.

Demon 1: You name it. These kids have done it in their churches.

Satan: I know the target group. I'm the one who requested the statistics. What are the results? I can't wait a minute longer. Read them to me!

Demon 1: It will be our pleasure.

Demon 2: Two out of three kids admitted that they lied to their parents within the last three months.

Satan: Yes!

Demon 1: Fifty-nine percent said they lied to their peers.

Satan: Excellent!

Demon 2: Nearly 45 percent watched MTV at least once a week.

Satan: And they said it was a fad!

Demon 1: One in three said they've cheated on exams.

Demon 2: Nearly one in four have smoked.

Demon 1: One in five tried to physically hurt someone.

Satan: Amazing!

Demon 1: One in nine have gotten drunk.

Demon 2: Nearly one in ten have used illegal drugs!

Demon 1: As an added bonus, over half of them feel confused and stressed out. Confusion reigns!

Satan: And I am the author of it. Give me the report, and return to the battlefield. Much to do, comrades! Steal, kill, destroy! Seek and devour! Let's rob their joy!

Written by Matt Tullos © 2001 LifeWay Christian Resources

Discuss the python story on page 42. Ask, **Have you ever known someone who was struggling for his or her spiritual life like the man in Texas struggled for his life and lost it?**

If possible, form six small groups (at least four students per group). If you don't have enough students, form as many small groups as you can. Allow one student from each group to select a topic from this list:

The Spirit of Jealousy (p. 43)	The Spirit of Lying (p. 44)
The Spirit of Perversion (p. 45)	The Spirit of Pride (p. 47)
The Spirit of Bondage (p. 48)	The Spirit of Witchcraft (p. 49)

Ensure each group has a different topic. Ask them to spend a few minutes in small groups reading about their topic. Then ask them to creatively report on how this spirit infiltrates a teen's life. They could do this using diagrams, improv, illustration, Scripture search, mime, or any other medium. Tip: Have adults facilitate these small groups and ask them to think of some ideas they could contribute if the students need assistance.

Allow time for each group to make presentations. After the presentations, communicate to the large group that Satan doesn't always appear as something really scary or evil, but he entices us into spiritual wickedness. He comes to us as a wolf in sheep's clothing: *"Watch out for false prophets. They come to you in sheep's clothing, but inwardly they are ferocious wolves" (Matt. 7:15).*

Get two volunteers to read the following short biblical illustration.

BIBLICAL ILLUSTRATION

Reader 1: *(as Satan)* Hey, Eve.
Reader 2: *(as Eve)* Who are you?
Reader 1: Just a friend. Pretty cool place.
Reader 2: Sure is.
Reader 1: It's all yours, isn't it?
Reader 2: I guess so. God gave it to me and Adam.
Reader 1: The whole place? And you can eat anything you want?
Reader 2: Sure. Almost anything.
Reader 1: What? Did I hear you say "almost"? What do you mean "almost"?

Reader 2: Well there is that tree over there.

Reader 1: What about it?

Reader 2: Well...

Reader 1: You're not going to eat the fruit off that tree?

Reader 2: But everything else is–

Reader 1: Wait a minute. You can't let Him do that! You have rights.

Reader 2: But God loves me, and I'm sure that–

Reader 1: Some love, huh? He won't even trust you with a little morsel of fruit. Look at the sign, Eve! Knowledge of good and evil....He doesn't want you to eat it because He thinks He's better than you. He doesn't love you! He wants to rule you! Taste it, Eve.

Reader 2: What?

Reader 1: Taste the fruit! Now!

Reader 2: Let me talk to Adam first.

Reader 1: I can't believe it! When are women going to stand up and think for themselves? Eat it. It will make you wise. Take charge of your own life.

After the sketch, read the last paragraph on page 50.

Lead the group into a time of silent prayer. Instruct students to ask God to reveal the strongholds in their lives. After a few moments, ask, **Would you like to share about the battles you are fighting?** Allow the students to express freely their confessions, and ask them to support each other during this time. As students and adults confess their struggles, stop after each one and ask a friend of theirs to pray publicly for them.

Option: Ask the adults to be prepared to pray for the persons who share struggles. This might work best in more intimate small groups.)

Be prepared for this session to go longer than the usual meeting. If God moves in your group, don't allow any schedule to detract you from the discoveries and confessions that are being made. We must not grieve the Holy Spirit through our own time limitations and church meeting schedules. Alert anyone who may be concerned by a possible extended session. If you let them know ahead of time about the possible conflicts and why they might occur, they'll probably be respectful of the experience. You may finish the session on time, but it is better to prepare than to apologize later.

After the session winds down, ask the students to turn to the last page of the session, A Commitment of My Spirit (p. 51). Have a volunteer read this statement and then challenge the students to commit to spiritual purity, which ultimately leads to pure joy.

Invite students to clip the coupon for Pure Spirit on page 77. Encourage them to place it in their Bible or on their mirror as a reminder of their quest for purity of the mind.

SESSION FIVE

Things You'll Need
❏ note cards with names of body parts
❏ paper and pens
❏ Where's Waldoff? (p. 91)
❏ Desperately Seeking Suzanne (p. 91)

As students arrive, give each of them a card with one of the following body parts on it: Hands; Eyes; Torso; Legs; Head; Feet. (For a smaller group decrease the number of body parts.) Have the students find others with the same body part and sit together. These will be the small groups.

Read Kerry's journal entry on page 52. Each group is to write a letter that would encourage and give wise counsel to Kerry. Instruct them to give her advice and help from Scripture. They can be creative and incorporate advice concerning their group's body part. After five minutes, allow a volunteer from each group to read his or her group's letter aloud. Then ask everyone, **Do you know anyone that reminds you of Kerry? Do you ever find yourself in Kerry's position?**

GROUP WORK

Divide the group into a guys group and a girls group. Say: **Your group is going to help two fictional characters, Waldoff and Suzanne, plan their weekly schedules. I will give you a list of activities to include in the schedule. Don't forget about time for meals, sleep, and time with God.**

Where's Waldoff?
Radio Station Internship 3 hours a week (flexible)
Waiter at Gary's Grill 3:00-8:00 p.m. Three times a week
School 7:30 a.m.-3:00 p.m.
Church Discipleship 6:30-8:00 p.m. Wednesday
Girlfriend
School Soccer Practice 90 minutes on Monday and Wednesday
Regular Worship Attendance
Dog—responsibilities to walk, feed, and train

Desperately Seeking Suzanne
First Priority at school 7:00-7:25 a.m. Monday-Friday
School 7:30 a.m.-3:00 p.m.
Worship Team Practice 7:00-8:00 p.m. Wednesday
School Band 3:30-4:30 p.m. Monday, Tuesday, Wednesday
Babysitting 6:00-8:00 p.m. Tuesday and Thursday
Yearbook Staff 3:00-4:30 p.m. Thursday
Homework
Regular Worship Attendance
Chores at home—laundry and cooking two nights a week

Ask the groups, **What is the physical downside to that kind of lifestyle?** *(Possible Answers: bad diet, stress on the body, lack of time to exercise, sleep depravation)*

Ask for volunteers to find and read aloud the following Scriptures:
   1 Corinthians 6:19   *Matthew 26:41*
   Proverbs 14:30   *2 Corinthians 4:10*

Review the Five Threats to Pure Joy in the body (pp. 53-62) using the following questions for discussion:

Threat 1
• How could busyness be considered a false God?
• Why is it hard to say no to opportunities that come your way?
• Does being spiritual mean saying yes to every ministry opportunity?

Threat 2
• What happens to the Christian who doesn't get enough exercise?

- Can exercise be an aid to worship? *(Yes! Some of the best prayer experiences can happen when you are jogging alone.)*

Threat 3
- Is appetite the only reason why people eat?
- Why is an eating disorder centrally a control issue?
- What would you say to a friend who might have an eating disorder?
- Is eating ever a part of worshiping God?

Threat 4
- Why are students today still users even though they are more educated about the effects of drugs than they were a few years ago?
- What does Ephesians 5:18 teach about alcohol?

Threat 5
- How is it possible that sexual sin is not only a sin against the mind, will, and emotions, but also a sin against the body?
- What plans are destroyed by premarital sex?
- After indulging in sensual flesh acts, what is harder for us to get: forgiveness from God or forgiveness from self? Who is the one who can't forget: God or self?

Ask the students to turn to the last page of the session, A Commitment of My Body (p. 62). Have a volunteer read this statement. Challenge the students to commit to purity of their body, which ultimately leads to pure joy.

Invite students to clip the coupon for Pure Body (p. 77), place it in a prominent place, and reflect on all four commitments during the week.

SESSION SIX

Things You'll Need
❑ candles and matches
❑ large cross
❑ one or two students prepared to share a testimony of God's work in their life during the study
❑ PowerPoint, marker board, or poster with marker

The final session of *Pure Joy* is the most important, yet the simplest. We aren't going to give you a list of game ideas and visual options for this session. This is where the *Pure Joy* experience turns toward a passionate worship experience, the culmination of everything the group has encountered so far.

Before the students arrive, create a unique environment by using candles for lighting. If candles are your only lighting source, have plenty of them to provide light for students to read and write. Remove all the chairs from the meeting room. Lay a large, authentic-looking cross in the middle of the meeting room.

Ask arriving students to enter worshipfully. Invite them to sing a few familiar worship choruses, a cappella.

Ask the enlisted students to share what God has done in their lives during the *Pure Joy* study. Allow time for others to share.

Direct the students' attention to the cross and tell them to think about what the cross of Christ means to them. Offer them a chance to share some of their thoughts.

Read the journal entry on page 65. Explain that God's joy and passion are waiting for us if we will only embrace the cross.

Ask them to think about how they would describe their spiritual state right now. Tell them not to respond aloud, but to meditate and reflect on where they are tonight.

Read *Matthew 11:28-30* to the group. Ask: **Where does God want you to be spiritually? How does it differ from your spiritual state right now?** Allow students to share their answers with the group.

Read step 3 in the book on page 68. Ask, **Is there anyone here who has learned during this study why they act and react certain ways?** *(Possible answer: I cling to people because I'm afraid of the feeling of rejection I felt when my parents divorced.)*

Lead the group in a time of silent prayer. Give students enough time to confess their own prayers. During this time have three adults read these Scriptures: *Psalm 38:18; 1 John 1:9; Psalm 51:4.*

Lead the group in another time of worship and singing.

Define *spiritual strongholds* (p. 70). Ask a leader to give an example of how God delivered him from a spiritual stronghold in his life.

Ask the students, **Has God been working in your life to remove spiritual strongholds?**

After students respond, take time to pray for them. Ask a student or adult to lead the group in these prayers. Invite them to use the example prayer on page 70 as a guide for these prayers. Don't treat this prayer as some kind of *secret recipe* prayer. Remind students that God is listening to the cries of their hearts.

Talk them through the process of releasing forgiveness and receiving forgiveness, as found on pages 70-72.

Ask a student to read *Mark 11:25.*

Read *Psalm 149:6.* Communicate to the students that praise is a powerful weapon against the powers of the enemy, Satan. The very mention of the name of Jesus causes Satan's militia to tremble in their boots!

End by leading students into a spontaneous worship experience. Invite them to read a passage of Scripture to the group, to begin singing a familiar worship song, to share a testimony, or to lead in prayer.

Display in large print *Romans 8:1-2.*

Ask them to repeat it and let the words of the truth sink into their spirits.

Communicate to the group the importance of finding one or two others of the same sex to serve as accountability partners. Remind them that the battle for purity is ongoing, and they will need others to strengthen them and to pray for them.

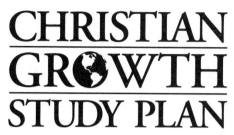

CHRISTIAN GROWTH
STUDY PLAN
Preparing Christians to Serve

In the Christian Growth Study Plan, this book *Pure Joy* is a resource for course credit in the subject area "Personal Life" of the Christian Growth category of diploma plans. To receive credit, youth should attend the four study sessions from this book. Duplicate a copy of the form on the next page for each student and complete the information.

Send the completed page to: Christian Growth Study Plan, One LifeWay Plaza, Nashville, TN 37234-0117. FAX: (615)251-5067

For information about the Christian Growth Study Plan, refer to the current Christian Growth Study Plan Catalog. Your church office may have a copy. If not, request a free copy from the Christian Growth Study Plan office (615)251-2525. Also available online at www.lifeway.com/cgsp/catalog.

Pure Joy: God's Formula for Passionate Living
CG–0790

PARTICIPANT INFORMATION

Social Security Number (USA ONLY-optional)

_ _ _ – _ _ – _ _ _ _

Personal CGSP Number*

_ _ – _ _ _ _

Date of Birth (MONTH, DAY, YEAR)

_ _ – _ _ – _ _

Name (First, Middle, Last)

Home Phone

_ _ _ – _ _ _ _

Address (Street, Route, or P.O. Box)

City, State, or Province

Zip/Postal Code

CHURCH INFORMATION

Church Name

Address (Street, Route, or P.O. Box)

City, State, or Province

Zip/Postal Code

CHANGE REQUEST ONLY

☐ Former Name

☐ Former Address

City, State, or Province

Zip/Postal Code

☐ Former Church

City, State, or Province

Zip/Postal Code

Signature of Pastor, Conference Leader, or Other Church Leader

Date

*New participants are requested but not required to give SS# and date of birth. Existing participants, please give CGSP# when using SS# for the first time. Thereafter, only one ID# is required. **Mail to:** Christian Growth Study Plan, One LifeWay Plaza, Nashville, TN 37234-0117. Fax: (615)251-5067.

Rev. 10-01